To Megan,

He is faithful!

♡,

Amber Gallagher

Ps. 34:5

Searching for Happily *Ever* After

A Companion for The Lady Who Waits

AMBER GALLAGHER

Copyright © 2013 AMBER GALLAGHER.

All rights reserved. No part of this book may be used or reproduced by any means, graphic, electronic, or mechanical, including photocopying, recording, taping or by any information storage retrieval system without the written permission of the publisher except in the case of brief quotations embodied in critical articles and reviews.

WestBow Press books may be ordered through booksellers or by contacting:

WestBow Press
A Division of Thomas Nelson
1663 Liberty Drive
Bloomington, IN 47403
www.westbowpress.com
1-(866) 928-1240

Because of the dynamic nature of the Internet, any web addresses or links contained in this book may have changed since publication and may no longer be valid. The views expressed in this work are solely those of the author and do not necessarily reflect the views of the publisher, and the publisher hereby disclaims any responsibility for them.

Any people depicted in stock imagery provided by Thinkstock are models, and such images are being used for illustrative purposes only.

Certain stock imagery © Thinkstock.

ISBN: 978-1-4497-9107-0 (sc)
ISBN: 978-1-4497-9108-7 (hc)
ISBN: 978-1-4497-9106-3 (e)

Library of Congress Control Number: 2013906392

Printed in the United States of America.

WestBow Press rev. date: 6/12/2013

Scripture taken from the HOLY BIBLE, NEW INTERNATIONAL VERSION® NIV® Copyright © 1973, 1978, 1984, 2011 Biblica. Used by permission. All rights reserved worldwide.

Scripture taken from the New King James Version. (NKJV) Copyright © 1982 by Thomas Nelson, Inc. Used by permission. All rights reserved.

Scripture taken from The Message. (MSG) Copyright © 1993, 1994, 1995, 1996, 2000, 2001, 2002. Used by permission of NavPress Publishing Group.

Scripture quotations marked NLT are taken from the Holy Bible, New Living Translation, copyright © 1996, 2004, 2007 by Tyndale House Foundation. Used by permission of Tyndale House Publishers, Inc., Carol Stream, Illinois 60188. All rights reserved.

Scripture is taken from GOD'S WORD®, ©1995 God's Word to the Nations. Used by permission of Baker Publishing Group.

Scripture taken from the NEW AMERICAN STANDARD BIBLE®, Copyright © 1960, 1962, 1963, 1968, 1971, 1972, 1973, 1975, 1977, 1995 by the Lockman Foundation. Used by permission.

Scripture quotations marked HCSB are taken from the Holman Christian Standard Bible®, Copyright © 1999, 2000, 2002, 2003, 2009 by Holman Bible Publishers. Used by permission. Holman Christian Standard Bible®, Holman CSB®, and HCSB® are federally registered trademarks of Holman Bible Publishers.

Scripture taken from the King James Version of the Bible.

Author image by Kristen Tackett, www.kristenmariephotos.wix.com

*To all the ladies-in-waiting
who are searching for happily-ever-after,
and to those who are afar off...
You are so dear to my heart.*

Acknowledgments

Thank you to my King. You have been wooing me my whole life. Thank you for never giving up on me and for that invitation to join in The Great Legacy Love Affair adventure with You. It has been my joy. You will always be the Love of my life.

Thank you to my husband, Brian Gallagher. You are such a wonderful husband with a love for God that moves me. You are my hero and I love you!

Thank you to my grandparents and my parents and to all of my family and friends who have without reservation been my biggest encouragers. My cup runneth over! Thank you for being excited with me and for holding my hands through the joys and struggles that provided the material for this book all these years later.

Thank you to Melissa Brickner for always agreeing to be the first to read my writing ventures. I couldn't have done this without you. Your input was amazingly helpful. You are so good to me and I am grateful for you.

Thank you to the Community Pregnancy Center Board and Staff. I am grateful for your support, encouragement, friendship, leadership, and training as I learned how to be a woman in ministry.

Contents

Once Upon a Time: *An Introduction* xiii

The Great Legacy Love Affair

1. The Great Legacy Love Affair 3
2. Oh, How He Loves You and Me: *Understanding the Heart of a King* 7
3. Every Great Love Story 13
4. To Be or Not to Be a Princess 21

The Lady-in-Waiting

5. The Lady-in-Waiting 31
6. What Does a Lady Do During the Wait? 41
7. Fall in Love with Your First Love 45
8. Find the Treasure in Singleness 57
9. Determine God's Dreams for You 63
10. Become the Woman You Long to Be 77
11. Be A Part of Your Love Story . . . *Long Before Your Prince Ever Comes* 85

Purity and Relationships

12. Abstinence Makes the Heart Grow Fonder 95
13. Purity Is a Lifestyle 115

14. Conquering Temptation...123
15. The Mystery Behind Purity..135
16. How Do I Know He's "The One"?...143
17. Courtship: *Is It the Same as Dating?*..................................149
18. Hearing God's Voice...161

The Wait

19. When Dreams Die: *Surviving a Devastated Heart*..........177
20. When the Wait Is Hard: *Sowing and Reaping*...............189
21. Sowing Seeds: *January 18, 1995 to January 27, 2003*.......193
22. The Rain: *August 9, 2003 to June 13, 2006*......................199
23. Harvest Is Coming: *September 4, 2006 to July 16, 2009*....209
24. Songs of Joy: *August 2, 2009 to October 5, 2010*..........225

When Dreams Come True

25. You've Got Mail!...245
26. The Lady in the Red Coat..251
27. "I Still Love You!"..255
28. New Year's Eve and Family Ties..261
29. True Love and Carriage Rides...267
30. A God-Sized Tale..273

Happily-Ever-After: *An Epilogue*..279
Endnotes..283
About Amber Gallagher...289

Once Upon a Time

An Introduction

Your eyes saw my unformed body; all the days ordained for me were written in your book before one of them came to be. (Psalm 139:16 NIV)

Once upon a time—doesn't that little phrase draw you into a tale with the expectation of adventure? Every time I hear it, I am usually hooked until I have read the thing through. As an avid reader, I must say that I certainly appreciate a good story.

If God had told me how He was going to write my story, I would have been nervous! It is certainly not a story that I would have written for myself. Sadly, I would have written out all of the trials and pain and kept what I would have considered good according to my own small-minded judgment. What a travesty that would have been. In my foolishness, I would have erased the very events that caused me to drop to my knees and lift up my eyes beyond the ordinary and dare to dream of the extraordinary for my life. In my rendition of a perfectly written happily-ever-after, I would have missed the real "Once Upon a Time," when a King left His throne to save a desperate people in waiting. My ears would have been deaf to His words comforting me and giving me hope of things yet to come. I believe that it was in my lack that I understood Who I really needed after all. I am eternally grateful that God wrote this story and I did not. He is masterful at weaving adventure, intrigue, and of course, a variety of surprising plot twists in every chapter. I've been on the edge of my seat for about thirty-four years now.

Daughter of the King, God has a story for you, too. Our heavenly Father rules over a great Kingdom and a continuing story of which you, dear lady, are very much a part. You might wonder where your adventure is taking you, but even though the middle of the story may seem frightening or hopeless, I assure you that when He ties the details together, the tale is sure to take your breath away! Your story is going to end well because those are the kind that the Master Storyteller writes.

But will you let Him? You can write your own life story, but it will not be as intensely adventurous, powerful or thrilling as it is when God holds the pen. I have lived it both ways.

Several years ago, I suffered through a disappointing time of shattered hope, and cried out to God, "Why am I here?" In this state of desperation, I heard Him say to me, "Show them how to love Me." I believe that He was talking about you.

Often, God allows me to cross paths with young ladies who are in a place that I remember all too well. They desperately want to trust the Lord for His plan in their lives and relationships. They are precious daughters of The Great King, looking for encouragement in a world filled with "give it to me now." They are choosing to WAIT. Unfortunately, many women these days squirm at this little four-letter word. Most do not want to wait—for anything. We want our food fast, our entertainment constant, and our husbands NOW! Please understand that fast does not mean better. Too often, quick and desperate seeking will produce slow and desperate results.

Early in life I became dissatisfied with "good enough" and extremely weary of a culture trying to pressure me to settle for it. I am grateful that I was raised in a preacher's home and at the age of five years old accepted Christ as my Savior. I seriously cannot remember a time when I did not love the idea of Jesus. I was one of those little wide-eyed preschoolers who believed that the deacon playing Jesus in the annual Easter play was the real deal and couldn't help but follow him around until it was time to close the sanctuary doors after a weekend of performances.

In my preteen years, I immersed myself in youth group activities. These were my people. After one particular youth service dealing with the importance of purity, I made a commitment to abstain from the party scene and all the trappings that came with it. In a dramatic conclusion, we were called on to literally stand if we were serious in making a commitment to save sexual activity until marriage. I stood that day having no idea that this decision would not only affect what lunch table I sat at in junior high, but also that it would become a passion and future ministry. The preacher had talked about God's plan for our relationships that night and it made sense. Before that time, although uncertain as to how to obtain it, I knew for certain that I longed to have an amazing love story.

I found a couple of my old journal entries the other day that made me smile:

1/1/93 Amber age 14

I watched the movie 'Wild Hearts Can't Be Broken.' Sometimes I wish I could meet a guy like she did. It's so romantic.

2/5/93

I pray that God will protect my husband and teach him the way he is supposed to live.

Even at fourteen years old, something in me persisted in believing that God could write this kind of story. Along the way, God has graciously shown me valuable truths during the triumphs and the failures—all in the hands of a loving Father. Yes, the path is narrow but also more adventurous with many treasures awaiting those willing to see them. Would you let me come alongside you, perhaps as a spiritual sister? I would like to encourage you to embrace this waiting time. While your steps may be uncertain, the dance is quite beautiful.

How can a man or woman have the living God come to live within and the result not be extraordinary? And yet so many Christians manage to live very small run-of-mill lives. They do not see how beautiful they are in Christ—how overwhelmingly loved . . . how rich with potential and purpose and power. The fact of the matter is that we are all extraordinary in God. But only a few have the faith to see it, and even fewer are brazen enough to act as though it is true.

-Michael Warden, *Alone With God*[1]

The Great Legacy Love Affair

1

The Great Legacy Love Affair

Instead of hopeless, I'd much rather view myself as a "hopeful" romantic. My sentimental heart was in full bloom even as a little girl watching the classics like "Cinderella" or "Snow White," and playing with one of my dearest friends. Her name was Barbie and she was from a faraway land called Mattel.® We managed countless adventures together without ever leaving my room and even though my family moved around a lot, Barbie and I never had to say goodbye as was the case with my other friends. She was always ready to follow me anywhere. One of my favorite ways to spend an afternoon would involve dreaming up a big adventure where through a series of mishaps Barbie would find herself in distress. She would call for help and just in time, our prince (Rock Star Ken, in this case) would come to the rescue riding—yes, you guessed it—on a white horse. I cannot tell you how many times I had Barbie rehearse our little drama. Somehow, the story never got old.

I fail to remember when it was that I put Barbie in her case for the last time, but I know that there came a time when it was not considered mature anymore to go around using your Barbie dolls to dramatize your own longed-for fairytale.

Along the way, a few broken hearts and well-meaning "encouragers" bade me to understand clearly that life is not a fairytale and happily-ever-afters simply do not exist in the real world. Outwardly, it seemed as if what they were saying was true, but secretly, I felt crushed. No matter how hard I tried to let go of my happily-ever-after dreams, while I could bury them, they simply refused to die. It became only rarely that I would ponder the question that always seemed to invade my dreams, ". . . what if it were real?"

Then one day, Christ whispered to my heart and His words blew the doors off my imprisoned childhood dreams. It was then that I knew without a doubt that happily-ever-after was real after all, not merely for me, but for anyone who would be brave enough to search it out.

It is the glory of God to conceal a thing: but the honor of kings is to search out a matter. (Proverbs 25:2 KJV)

Jack and Helen Watkins

In June of 2000, I was a counselor at our church's summer youth camp. It was a tough week as I tried to deal with a genuinely broken heart. Our pastor's wife, Helen Watkins, had recently passed away due to heart complications. Several of us from the same church family left camp to attend her funeral. In the end, like the psalmist, I found myself "worn out with sobbing" and my pillow was continually "wet from weeping" (Psalm 6:6).

I wish you could have seen them together. Pastor Walter (Jack) Watkins and Helen truly loved each other. He was such a gentleman who spoke highly of his beloved wife and was the kind of man who would open car doors or take her hand to lead her up a flight of stairs. Pastor would often tell us stories about their love affair. My favorite was his recounting of a cinema-worthy tale in which he risked his life to save Helen from drowning in a raging river current. I loved to watch them together and couldn't help but notice that they would find little ways to show one another they cared.

Needless to say, I was pretty devastated when she passed away. It was Jack and Helen's love story to be sure, but that did not stop me from feeling as if I were in some way a part of it. I could always find myself invested into a good love story. Once, while seeing a movie with my mom, we had watched a wrenching love saga that ended with the hero dying. I cried so hard that people were turning around in their seats. I didn't mean to make a scene; I simply felt the loss as if it were my own, as was the case with the story of Jack and Helen. Their relationship profoundly moved me. It gave me hope that a beautiful love story was not merely found in books or movies, but could be obtainable in real life. I needed to believe this was true.

* * * *

Back at youth camp, the Thursday evening service was coming to a close. The young ladies I was chaperoning for the week had left their seats to go and pray at the altar. I stood up, readying myself to join them in prayer, when I heard the Lord say to me, "Stay here. I want to talk to you for a while."

At that point, I broke down and began to pour out my heart to the Lord asking every "why" question I could think of. "Why did Helen have to go? Pastor and Helen were my inspiration. Why now? Their love affair is a legacy. I will even tell my own children about the beautiful love story of Pastor Jack and Helen and how he saved her from that raging river long ago," I cried.

That's when I heard God say, "Amber, I want *our* love affair to be a legacy."

I was totally blown away. It took me a few days to get over the shock of such a personal encounter with God. I began to seek the Lord like never before, and He began to speak—or maybe I began to really listen as He unveiled, through the Word, His longing to have a love affair between Himself and His bride, which included me. He revealed to me what I have come to call "The Great Legacy Love Affair."

This encounter with God catapulted me into a journey that I am still on and loving to this day—a journey to discover the sacred heart of the Ancient of Days. This revelation of God's love was not solely for me, but for you too. It is vital for you as a daughter of The Great King, princess of heaven, to realize who you are to God and that you are the center of His affection. Only then can you truly know the immense value that you possess. Only when caught up in the eternal romance with The Great King can our hearts ever truly be satisfied.

He has made everything beautiful in its time. He has also set eternity in the hearts of men; yet they cannot fathom what God has done from beginning to end. (Ecclesiastes 3:11 NIV)

Oh, How He Loves You and Me

Understanding the Heart of a King

The servant girl stood on the auction block, shaking. She was covered in the mud and dust that comes with such a long journey. How things had drastically changed in her life. All that she had ever known to be safe and innocent had been stolen from her. When the enemy came to her village, he had spared nothing and no one. She had managed to escape only to be found hiding under a pile of wood and debris. Once the enemy and his soldiers had used her, they sold her to a traveling caravan of slave traders.

Now here she was. She no longer cared about or trusted anyone. This world she now faced did not leave room for that. As the bidding began, her mind started to wonder and became unsettled with the prospect of what may come. What if the man who purchased her wanted to use her as the enemy's soldiers had done? How could she bear it? She had a fleeting impulse to jump right off of the auction block and lunge toward the hills looming in the distance, but the chains on her feet would not allow her to even attempt it. Her mind raced frantically. "If only I could . . ."

That's when she saw him. She had heard the crowd gasp, but did not understand why. This man had bid on her and His bid was much too high a price for the young girl who looked like no more than a skeleton, for she was extremely thin and pale. He had outbid all the others by such an amount that they had all ceased their bidding. Who was this man with the kind eyes who had purchased her? She hardly knew, but for the first time in years, she wasn't afraid.

****

In our own way, you and I are that servant girl. Very early on in life, whether it was through the pain of abuse, rejection, abandonment or loneliness, we have all had to come face to face with what this world has to offer. For some of us, the pain has been intense, driving us to numbness or the refusal to trust.

However, if you truly search your heart, aren't you desperate for someone to rescue you because you are worth it? "Is there anyone brave enough or strong enough?" you may ask.

The answer is yes! There is One who knows you even better than you know yourself. He is strong enough and has *already* purchased your freedom with the price of His own bloodshed. His name is Jesus and He is the Christ, the Son of the living God!

We must understand God's heart toward us because, quite frankly, we will not trust someone we do not know and we will not love someone we do not trust. Therefore, it is essential for us to learn to trust in God's perfect love for us. He was brave enough to make the first move and He's been asking for your heart ever since.

For God so loved the world that he gave his one and only Son, that whoever believes in him shall not perish but have eternal life. (John 3:16 NIV)

Greater love has no one than this, that he lay down his life for his friends. (John 15:13 NIV)

When we were utterly helpless, Christ came at just the right time and died for us sinners. (Romans 5:6 NLT)

Yes, God loves you! So much that He gave you the most precious gift He could possibly give—His perfect Son, Jesus. God held nothing back from you.

The Bible calls Jesus, the "Lamb that was slain before the foundation of the world" (Revelation 13:8). Jesus knew what would need to be done to get to us even before we were created and He said "Yes." We know it was His choice because, leading up to His crucifixion, He lets the disciples know that "no one takes" His life from Him, rather he will lay His life down of His own choosing (John 10:18).

This truth causes me to recall a conversation I had about the love of Christ with a young woman who was a Buddhist. She was hurting over an experience where she had been miserably abused. She sought and could not find comfort. I told her about a precious King who chose to leave Heaven where He was celebrated in order to sacrifice his life to give her freedom and healing. In the end, I reasoned, "No one has ever loved me like that, but Jesus." She listened intently and let me pray with her after our conversation. I believe, perhaps for the first time in her life, she had come face to face with Love Himself.

Isn't it freeing to know that He willingly paid the price that only He, a perfect lamb, could pay in order to rescue us? My heart is forever captured by this truth. Someone who loves you that much could only have your good in mind. How could we not trust a God who gave everything for love of us?

At times that is hard to believe. We often see God through distorted glasses. Perhaps you may compare Him to your parents, authority figures, boyfriends or even abusers. Unfortunately, the problem with viewing God this way is that we humans may have been created in His image, but we are all flawed and will disappoint at one time or another. No one is like God. We only see glimpses of Him as in the kindness of a friend, the laughter of a baby or in the innocence of a child. These are only glimpses. They are not the complete picture of our amazing God who is perfectly pure, unselfishly loving, and abundantly servant-hearted. His heart toward us is good, not evil or manipulative.

He tells us in His Word that He has come that we would have "life abundantly" (John 10:10) and that "all things work for the good to them that love God and are the called according to His purpose" (Romans 8:28).

Not Even a "Goodbye!"

Of the few romantic relationships that I have experienced, there were only two I would consider healthy. Most of them I started with stars in my eyes. At first they seemed promising, but would later turn out to be painful and even abusive. I was desperately searching for love. The odd thing about these relationships was that in the end of EVERY one of them, the guy conveniently forgot to let me know it was over. I would time and again have to search the guy out only to hear him say what I knew was coming, "I don't want you anymore." Ouch! Goodbyes are hard enough, but to not have been given the courtesy of an explanation or a "see you later" was crushing. I now understand that the enemy wanted to target a calculated attack on my heart to skew how I viewed love.

I found it such a relief to realize that not only will God never withdraw His love from me without so much as a backward glance, but also that He will never let anything separate me from His love. Now that is a revelation that can set a girl free! In many instances, we are afraid to love or be loved because we do not want to be disappointed, but that is not an issue with God's love. It is not something that is given and then taken away when it doesn't suit Him anymore. Knowing this truth has personally brought my heart indescribable freedom. Dear sister, His love has always been and will never fail to remain. You may not always understand His ways, but His motive is always for love of you. Your heart is safe is His hands.

Once we realize these truths, even in disappointing circumstances, we become like Peter, who when Christ asked if he too would leave like all the other deserters, exclaimed, "Lord, to whom would we go?

You have the words that give eternal life" (John 6:68-69 NLT). He becomes our greatest desire and we simply cannot walk away from such True Love.

For I am persuaded that neither death nor life, nor angels nor demons, neither the present nor the future, nor any powers, ³⁹neither height nor depth, nor anything else in all creation, will be able to separate us from the love of God that is in Christ Jesus our Lord. (Romans 8:38-39 NIV)

Every Great Love Story

When I took voice lessons as a teenager, my teacher would have me sing classical music. Unfortunately, I much preferred a more contemporary style. However, when she would give me a song to learn and then tell me the story behind why the melody was written, I was captivated every time and she knew it. I would sing the tune with all the emotion and feeling I could muster as if it were written about my life. As previously mentioned, I couldn't help but immerse myself whenever I felt connected to a story. I was always longing to get caught up into a breathtaking adventure. Can you relate?

God has used my love of a great story to draw me to Him and to help me better understand His heart toward me. Therefore, you can imagine that "The Great Legacy Love Affair" left a life-changing impression on my soul.

The Elements of a Great Love Story

Have you ever noticed that a great love story includes certain common elements? When you think about it and compare, these elements are every bit as present in our love story with Christ.

As a matter of fact, the Lord once told me, "Amber, the Cinderella stories, the prince and the happily-ever-after . . . that is all about

Me!" Those fairytale stories were derived from the Original Story, the Greatest Love Story. It is about God and his love affair with His Bride—that's us!

When the Lord began to open up the scriptures to me and show me this Love Story He wanted to have with me, I was truly amazed.

This is the true fairytale—a much more breathtaking adventure than the ones we grow up on! I think perhaps it would be fitting to begin with Once Upon a Time . . .

He Noticed Me

We all know that the beginning of a great love story typically starts when the young man, perhaps a prince, notices the girl. Doesn't this heroine usually seem to be the most unlikely of ladies to be chosen? And that is what I love. Almost immediately, the young man will set out on the quest of letting the young lady know that he sees her. Do you realize that God is the God who sees you and I (Genesis 16:13)? He noticed us and weren't we the most unlikely people to capture His attention? We are desperately human, not even holy of our own doing, yet He still noticed us. I also found it beautifully fascinating to discover when it was that God noticed us:

Long before he laid down earth's foundations, he had us in mind, had settled on us as the focus of his love, to be made whole and holy by his love. Long, long ago he decided to adopt us into his family through Jesus Christ. (Ephesians 1:4-6 Message)

Long before we were even born, God decided He wanted us. Before our mistakes, before everything, He still chose us. I especially love this idea of being chosen, because I'll tell you more than once I was the last one chosen for the kickball team on the playground and many times, I was the one passed over by the boy I had a crush on, but not this time. I was chosen before time began. Doesn't that comfort you? Let it sink in. Say it out loud, I AM CHOSEN! Wow! That *is* powerful, isn't it?

This is a basic truth that we have to have at the core of our hearts, lest we fall over ourselves trying to obtain someone else's attention—oftentimes a person whose attention we would be better off without. When I finally realized that God had noticed me, it helped my heart, for the first time, to rest. I don't have to be consumed with turning a guy's head. I have turned not only the head, but the heart of the greatest King who ever was and is to come again!

He Asked Me to Be His

Another element of a good love story has to be that moment when the guy asks that special girl to be his. God has done this for you and me. Actually, He still calls us in such a personal way to come and know Him. Do you know that the Bible says that we do not even come to God unless His Holy Spirit woos (an old-fashioned word for seeking someone's affection) us? (See John 6:44.)

Come to me with your ears wide open. Listen, and you will find life. I will make an everlasting covenant with you. I will give you all the unfailing love I promised to David. (Isaiah 55:3 NLT)

He Rescued Me

Of course, a story has to have that nail-biting moment when the damsel gets herself into an unfortunate bout of distress. This is when the dashing young hero rushes onto the scene to thwart the evil villain or stepsister and he rescues the girl. I love this part! The romantic in me usually wants to jump out of my seat and scream, "YEAHHHH!" Christ, our Hero, has already performed the ultimate death-defying act in order to rescue us. He did this when He gave His life on the cross to cover our sin and then He beat death and arose from that grave alive and well. As if that were not enough, the rescuing doesn't end there. Our Savior continues to save us daily from the trappings of this world and oftentimes from ourselves by teaching us His ways and guiding us in His path. There is no other love story like this one.

But he was pierced for our rebellion, crushed for our sins. He was beaten so we could be whole. He was whipped so we could be healed. All of us, like sheep, have strayed away. We have left God's paths to follow our own. Yet the L*ord* *laid on him the sins of us all.* (Isaiah 53:5-6 NLT)

The God of peace will soon crush Satan under your feet. May the grace of our Lord Jesus be with you. (Romans 16:20 NLT)

He Will Come for Me on a White Horse

After my encounter with God in 2000, He continued to speak to me about "The Great Legacy Love Affair." As He compared my childhood fairytales to His real-life romance with me, I would feel Him further probe my ideas with questions like, "The prince on a white horse? Where do you think that came from?"

I think I replied once by saying something really intelligent like, "Um . . . Walt Disney?"

Not quite. The Lord took me first to the scripture in Revelation 19.

Then I saw heaven opened, and a ***white horse*** *was standing there. Its rider was named Faithful and True, for he judges fairly and wages a righteous war.* [12] *His eyes were like flames of fire, and on his head were many crowns. A name was written on him that no one understood except himself.* [16] *On his robe at his thigh was written this title:* ***King of all kings and Lord of all lords.*** (Revelation 19:11-12, 16 NLT, emphasis added)

"What?" I hadn't remembered my Bible saying that before. When the Lord reveals His truth, it certainly leaves a forever imprint on your heart. The Lord went on to show me that these little girl dreams were not manufactured by Disney or any other artist. These ideas and storylines were God's from the beginning. The longing I had for the prince on a white horse, castles, and happy endings were simply outlets He used to awaken my longing for Him. He is *The Prince* on the white horse who has loved us from the very beginning.

We Will Live Happily-Ever-After

Fairytales all have "happy endings," but the story of our love affair with God will never end. As a matter of fact, the Bible says, "No eye has seen, no ear has heard, and no mind has imagined what God has prepared for those who love him" (1 Corinthians 2:9 NIV). It is true! He rescued us and will come again that we may forever be with Him, the One our heart loves. In the end, dear sister, we will live happily-ever-after.

I heard a loud shout from the throne, saying, 'Look, God's home is now among his people! He will live with them, and they will be his people. God himself will be with them. ⁴He will wipe every tear from their eyes, and there will be no more death or sorrow or crying or pain. All these things are gone forever.' ⁵And the one sitting on the throne said, 'Look, I am making everything new!' And then he said to me, 'Write this down, for what I tell you is trustworthy and true.' ⁶And he also said, 'It is finished! I am the Alpha and the Omega—the Beginning and the End. To all who are thirsty I will give freely from the springs of the water of life. ⁷All who are victorious will inherit all these blessings, and I will be their God, and they will be my children.' (Revelation 21:3-7 NLT)

And they will see his face, and his name will be written on their foreheads. ⁵And there will be no night there—no need for lamps or sun—for the Lord

God will shine on them. And they will reign forever and ever. (Revelation 22:4-5 NLT)

It is also important for you to know that these steps that Jesus took to woo us were the Jewish customs that a young man would follow in order to propose to and actually marry the woman he wanted as his wife. We are loved and wanted by our Savior. Daughter of God, you belong here. This is the Great Romance that you were destined to enjoy.

I have risked my heart to discover that, without a doubt, there is a Great King, a beautiful mansion . . . ahem . . . I mean castle, and an amazing happily-ever-after for those who choose it. God desires for you to be His and to Him, you are the most beautiful—He calls you princess (Psalm 45:13). When He says it, it has to be true because He cannot lie. He's too pure for that. So, dear sister, are you ready? Don't be afraid. Can you hear Him whisper, "Come, learn of Me, and you will find rest for your longing heart"?

I hope you find this as exciting as I have found it to be. Our love story with God is the greatest, most thrilling love story ever told!

Hero

Lord, I'm standing here again
A child with heart in hand
Is it really true, will You rescue me, come save the day?
Cause I'm so tired, I'm so lost
I cry out to You, my God
And there You are, were You always standing there?
My Hero, My Hero
He's come with fire in His eyes

Lord, I'm standing here again
A lover with heart in hand
Is it really true, will You come for me, take me away?
I'm so captivated, I'm so lost in love
I cry out to You, my God
And there You are, were You always standing there?
My Hero, My Hero
He's come with longing in His eyes.

–Amber Gallagher, "Hero," 2006

4

To Be or Not to Be a Princess

The king is enthralled by your beauty; honor him, for he is your lord. All glorious is the princess within her chamber; her gown is interwoven with gold. In embroidered garments she is led to the king. (Psalm 45:11, 13-14a NIV 1984)

In 2001 a popular movie made its debut. "The Princess Diaries" was a modern Cinderella story based on the books by Meg Cabot. The heroine, Mia Thermopolis, is a teenager who is told by her estranged grandmother, Queen Clarisse of Genovia, that her father was a prince and that she is in fact a real princess, next in line as the Queen. Mia is shocked, but realizes this is every girl's dream. She accepts her grandmother's offer to take "princess lessons," going through makeovers and royal etiquette drills.

Eventually, the tension gets to her and we find her sitting in the high school principal's office trying to escape the paparazzi. Her mother and grandmother talk to Mia about accepting the role of princess, when her mother blurts out in exasperation, "Before this, Mia was just a normal girl."

Queen Clarisse replies to her matter-of-factly, "She has never been normal, she was born royal, but she can choose not to go through with this."

Now Mia is faced once again with the decision to say "yes" to her destiny as princess or decline and return to life as she has always known it.

I would propose that the same opportunity is true for you. You were never just a normal girl. You were born to be royal, but as with Mia, you have a choice to make. You can say "yes" to your destiny as princess, daughter of The Great King or decline and return to life as you have always known it.

You accept your role as daughter of The Great King when you accept and believe that Jesus Christ died for you on the cross to cleanse you of your sin and then confess Him to be your Lord. Everyone at a divine point in their history will face this decision. If at any time you feel that this is a decision you still need to make, may I take a moment to encourage you to dive into this love story with Christ. The following is a simple prayer you might want to use as a guide to ask Jesus into your life:

Jesus, I do believe that You came and died on the cross that I might be forgiven. I have made mistakes and until now I have not lived my life for You. I want to change. I ask You to forgive me, cleanse me, and give me a fresh start right now. Please walk with me and show me how to be a woman who follows You. I accept my destiny as Your daughter, a princess of The Great King.

More Than Skin Deep

When I was eleven years old, it began—a decade-long battle for beautiful, smooth, and clear skin. You see, I was *blessed* with oily skin. Many people tried to console a miserable little girl ridden with acne by saying, "One day your face will clear up and that oily skin will cause you to get fewer wrinkles when you're old."

"Thanks, but what about now?" I would mutter under my breath.

There were times I didn't even want to leave my house. The kids at school were not exactly nice about it. Not only did I feel embarrassed, but I had painful cystic acne. It plain hurt! When picture time rolled around for the yearbook, I would try to think of ways to get out of it. Mornings would find me looking into the mirror with tear-brimmed eyes. What a time that was!

They were right. My face did begin to clear when I was in my twenties. The battle did leave behind a few scars, but through the pain, I gained valuable lessons in humility and a front-row seat in discovering one of my first disheartening realities about this culture. It is pretty superficial, mostly focused on outward appearance. Many people truly believe that beauty is *only* skin deep.

The Longing to Be Noticed

Many women, young and old, dream that someone will notice them for the beauty that is uniquely theirs. We will often buy into the myth that certain hairstyles, make-up, shampoo, revealing clothes or flawless skin will do the trick. The media especially loves to perpetuate this type of thinking. They will use sex appeal to sell everything from lipstick to hubcaps producing an airbrushed, false sense of "beauty" to manipulate guys and girls alike into buying what they have to sell. Sadly, women, young and old, have bought into this lie and will do the same, using sex appeal, lust, and manipulation in order to fabricate a false sense of intimacy from a young man. Beware! The femininity of a woman is a powerful gift from God. It can certainly be used for good or all kinds of evil.

I desperately longed to be thought of as beautiful, which left me open to being influenced in all the wrong directions. I eventually had to cut out of my life the magazines and movies that incessantly promoted this false sense of beauty and further encouraged me to use my femininity to manipulate others. I had found myself caught up by the clothes, make-up, and hair that the latest celebrities said were popular and trendy. I finally came to the conclusion that I didn't want these "godless wonders" to have such an influence over my thoughts and opinions. I wanted that to come from another Source—the truth of God's powerful Word.

We have established the fact that you, dear sister, have already been noticed. It happened long before the worlds were even created. God noticed and decided to love you extravagantly. He is our Creator and He alone has the authority and knowledge to tell you exactly how beautiful you really are.

In the movie, "The Princess Diaries," I understand that Mia needed help in learning the etiquette and protocols of royalty. However, what gave me pause was the age-old fascination with outward beauty that always seems to entangle us. The majority of Mia's "princess lessons" were spent giving Mia a makeover from head to toe. When the hair designer presents her to the Queen, he implies that now, only after extensive beauty treatments, can he present a princess.

Keep in mind that Mia was a princess because of who her father was and not because her hair was straightened and eyebrows tweezed.

Esther

This "beauty is only skin deep" line of thinking has been around for a long time. An ancient "Princess Diary" account is recorded in the book of Esther in the Old Testament. Esther was a young lady who lived a common life as she was being raised by her cousin, Mordecai. Then one day the King of the land, Xerxes, decided he wanted another wife. As a result of his whim, the officials rounded up all of the young virgins in the land, which included Esther.

These girls were then taken to the palace where they were given royal beauty treatments for a whole year before they could even meet the King. Even back then, the culture focused on outward beauty to make a princess (Esther 2:12). The great thing about Esther is that she seemed to win the affection of everyone around her, including those in charge and eventually above all the other maidens, she won the heart of the King. I'm sure Esther was beautiful like all the other maidens who were brought into the palace. However, I believe it was her character that separated her above all the rest, opening doors of friendship and favor. Esther's story describes a woman who is unselfish, humble, kind, self-controlled, brave, godly, and wise. Now that is the character of a beautiful princess.

God has quite a different standard for beauty than the world has. He is clear to reveal that the content of our heart is what produces a true beauty, which radiates from the inside out.

Samuel, Eliab, and David

The sixteenth chapter of the book of Samuel contains a story about a prophet for whom this book is named. Samuel was told by God to go to the house of a man named Jesse to anoint the next king of Israel. Samuel obeys and has Jesse line up all of his sons so that, one by one, Samuel can look them over to see which of them is to be king. The oldest son of Jesse, Eliab, was first in line. He was handsome and well built. Samuel thought for sure that this was God's choice. Eliab looked the part. Yet, God had other ideas about this tall, dark, and handsome young man. He instructs Samuel:

'Do not consider his appearance or his height, for I have rejected him. The LORD does not look at the things man looks at. Man looks at the outward appearance, but the LORD looks at the heart.' (1 Samuel 16:7b NIV)

An Ugly Heart Makes an Ugly Man

Eliab may have appeared to be fitted for the role of king, but God had rejected him. If you read further in this book of Samuel, you will find that Eliab was a hateful, critical, and jealous man. (See 1 Samuel 17:12-29.)

Samuel then surveys Jesse's other sons and God rejects all of them. I can imagine Samuel feeling a bit of confusion at this point as he asks Jesse if there is anyone missing. Jesse hesitates but eventually reveals to Samuel that he did have another son, David, who was in the fields, taking care of sheep. Jesse did not even bother to present this son as an option and yet when Samuel finally saw him, God immediately let Samuel know that David was to be the next king. David may not have "looked the part" to Samuel or even to his own father, but to God he was the beautiful fit. The Bible reveals David to be a "man after God's own heart" (Acts 13:22) and this young shepherd is eventually revered as the greatest human king in all of Israel's history. In addition, David happens to be an ancestor in the family tree of Jesus Christ.

So it is with a lady's beauty, which is not determined by any outward thing, but rather what is in her heart. When God's presence lives inside of you as His daughter, you carry Him who is the most beautiful, beloved, and sacred of all.

Now, I am not suggesting that you shouldn't dress nicely or brush your teeth and hair. I think we should strive to be excellent in all that we do, even in our appearance. After all, God displays excellence and order in absolutely everything He does. His beauty evokes our interest and excitement. Simply look at a crimson sunset or a mountainside of trees that have changed color in the fall.

A Priceless Treasure

One of my favorite things to do is travel. It is quite an experience to find myself wrapped up in the history of the different countries and cities I am visiting. As a memento of my travels, I started collecting teacups. I have teacups from several different countries as well as from other personal events that have been sentimental to me. Displayed in special places in my home, I enjoy bringing them out for important occasions, like having a tea party with my nieces. I take care of these teacups because I consider them little treasures and they mean something to me.

I tell you all of this because I want you to pause and think of something in your life that you consider valuable and precious to you.

Why do you think of this object as a treasure? Do you throw it under your bed or leave it lying around like an old coffee mug or do you keep it in a place of honor, guarded from being broken and abused?

Now that you know how beautiful and sacred you are to God, not an object but a treasured daughter, how do you think He desires that you view yourself? How do you think He expects others to treat you?

I know of a wise mother who wanted to find a way to teach her daughters how valuable they were to their parents and to God. She stood these little girls in front of an old china hutch that displayed beautiful, antique china. She reminded the girls that this fine china was valuable. They were not toys, but treasures presented on the most special of occasions. She went on to explain, "You are like fine china. Don't ever let anyone treat you like you're a disposable paper plate merely to be used up and thrown away."

A treasure is meant to be treated as something special, with care and consideration for its value, but sadly, many young ladies would treat a snow globe collection with more care and consideration than they would the treasures of their own heart, body or purity.

Ladies, you are extremely valuable and precious to the Lord. He created you to be His rare and delicate masterpiece. You don't have to pretend with Him. You don't have to devalue yourself to get noticed by Him. His eyes are on you and He is proud of what He sees. Remember that "the King is enthralled by your beauty" (Psalm 45:11).

I encourage you to accept your role as princess and I urge you to spend your time beautifying your heart instead of obsessing over your outward appearance.

Look at the birds. They don't plant or harvest or store food in barns, for your heavenly Father feeds them. And aren't you far more valuable to him than they are? (Matthew 6:26 NLT)

The Lady-in-Waiting

5

The Lady-in-Waiting

I shall be telling this with a sigh
Somewhere ages and ages hence:
Two roads diverged in a wood, and I—
I took the one less traveled by,
And that has made all the difference.

-Robert Frost, "The Road Not Taken"[1]

Enter through the narrow gate. For wide is the gate and broad is the road that leads to destruction, and many enter through it. [14]*But small is the gate and narrow the road that leads to life, and only a few find it.* (Matthew 7:13-14 NIV 1984)

If you have picked up this book, you are probably one of the brave ones who has determined or at least you are thinking about letting God have control of your life and love story. The adventure of waiting for the man that God has for you to marry can certainly seem like a long, stretched-out road at times. What does a lady do while waiting for her love story to begin?

Have you ever considered that you are already living in a chapter of your love story? Once, when I was praying about my future husband, the Lord whispered softly to my heart. "Amber," He said, "this time in your life is part of your love story." He went on to explain to me that many of us "wish away" our current lives as we eagerly wait for high school and then we cannot wait until college. We are obsessed about getting a better job and then eager to find our husbands and shortly after wish we had babies. Oh, how much we miss when we do this! Life is full of opportunities and experiences. God helped me to stop and open my eyes to see that in every season of my life, He has something special for me to do and to be. I wouldn't want to miss out on any of it as I anticipate the next chapter of my life.

Some women believe that they cannot branch out in ministry until their husbands come along. It could be that right now, you are called to a ministry opportunity temporarily—one that you have been specifically anointed to accomplish at this present time or perhaps He is using this time to prepare you for the next page in your storyline. Better still, could it be that He is accomplishing both of these purposes in your current situation?

Either way, you certainly don't want to miss a moment of what God has for you. Instead of dwelling on how your life is supposed to look ten years from now, why not ask the Lord to show you the purpose for this particular span on the timeline of your history? Once He shows you, make sure you get into what He is doing. You will be able to look back with satisfaction and accomplishment knowing that you used every moment in your life to fulfill God's will for you.

Paul

Take a look at Saul, whose name was changed to Paul on the Damascus Road when he had a life-changing encounter with Jesus Christ (Acts 9). He immediately set out to preach the gospel of Jesus to the Jews and they tried to kill him (Acts 9:29-30). Fourteen years passed before Paul began the public ministry of passionately preaching the gospel to the Gentiles (non-Jews).[2]

After his near-death encounter, he fled to another country. Paul states that it pleased God to "reveal his Son . . . so that I would proclaim the Good News about Jesus to the Gentiles." He further explains that after his conversion, he "did not rush out to consult with any human being, nor did I go up to Jerusalem to consult with those who were apostles before I was. Instead, I went away into Arabia, and later I returned to the city of Damascus" (Galatians 1:15b-17).

Each of these seasons—conversion, training, and public ministry—were vitally important in Paul's life. I can imagine that during those fourteen years before Paul was in full-time ministry, he was building spiritual muscles in order to have the ability to shoulder the responsibilities God was going to lay on him in the future.

You may find that you are in precisely the same place in your own life. Please don't lose sight of promises and dreams being fulfilled in this stage of your life too. These things have been specifically carved out for these particular days in your lifetime. It's not wrong to hope for the future that God has for you, but keep in mind that anticipating does no good if we are squandering the present, not fully redeeming the time we are given now. This tragic mistake can certainly delay and can severely hinder any future promise.

Parable of the Talents

Again, the Kingdom of Heaven can be illustrated by the story of a man going on a long trip. He called together his servants and entrusted his money to them while he was gone. [15] *He gave five bags of silver to one, two bags of silver to another, and one bag of silver to the last—**dividing it in proportion to their abilities**. He then left on his trip.*

[16] *The servant who received the five bags of silver began to invest the money and earned five more.* [17] *The servant with two bags of silver also went to work and earned two more.* [18] *But the servant who received the one bag of silver dug a hole in the ground and hid the master's money.*

[19]After a long time their master returned from his trip and called them to give an account of how they had used his money. [20]The servant to whom he had entrusted the five bags of silver came forward with five more and said, 'Master, you gave me five bags of silver to invest, and I have earned five more.'

[21]The master was full of praise. 'Well done, my good and faithful servant. You have been faithful in handling this small amount, so now I will give you many more responsibilities. Let's celebrate together!'

[22]The servant who had received the two bags of silver came forward and said, 'Master, you gave me two bags of silver to invest, and I have earned two more.' [23]The master said, 'Well done, my good and faithful servant. You have been faithful in handling this small amount, so now I will give you many more responsibilities. Let's celebrate together!'

[24]Then the servant with the one bag of silver came and said, 'Master, I knew you were a harsh man, harvesting crops you didn't plant and gathering crops you didn't cultivate. [25]I was afraid I would lose your money, so I hid it in the earth. Look, here is your money back.'

[26]But the master replied, 'You wicked and lazy servant! If you knew I harvested crops I didn't plant and gathered crops I didn't cultivate, [27]why didn't you deposit my money in the bank? At least I could have gotten some interest on it.'

*[28]Then he ordered, 'Take the money from this servant, and give it to the one with the ten bags of silver. [29]**To those who use well what they are given, even more will be given, and they will have an abundance.** But from those who do nothing, even what little they have will be taken away. [30]Now throw this useless servant into outer darkness, where there will be weeping and gnashing of teeth.'* (Matthew 25:13-30 NLT, emphasis added)

Jesus told this story of three servants who were given silver. The King James Version refers to this silver as "talents." Consider that these "talents" represent our "talents and abilities" given to us from the Lord. We all have different gifts and abilities, treasures if you will, to further Christ's kingdom here on Earth. Some of us encourage, preach, teach, listen, give abundantly, etc. Look at verses twenty-nine and thirty. If you use the talent and ability that God has given you, you will multiply the kingdom and will have served a divine purpose here with your time on this planet. On the other hand, if you view God as harsh and uncaring, refusing to serve Him, then you gain no one for Christ and do nothing to enhance His kingdom on Earth. The sad outcome means you will forfeit the Heavenly reward of spending eternity with God. He is the One with whom your heart was made to spend forever. What a tragedy!

Every day is precious, holding valuable opportunities to change this world using the abilities God has given to us. Let us use the time and our talents wisely.

David

Before he was the beloved king of Israel, David was misunderstood, passed over by those closest to him, and even hunted down like a deer running for his life. Remember that he was anointed to be the next king of Israel while he was still a shepherd boy and the current king was still reigning. Talk about an opportunity for jealousy and hatred.

The current king, Saul, had disobeyed God and He was getting ready to oust him and put David in his place. If you read further into David's "waiting time," you will see that he even had an opportunity to protect himself and take his role as king earlier than he did, by killing Saul. Saul pursued David and was in the midst of trying to wipe him out when the presiding king decided to take rest in a cave. Unknown to Saul, David and his men were back in that cave hiding out. As Saul is relieving himself, David slips up next to him and cuts off a part of Saul's robe. Take a look at the passage in 1 Samuel 24: 5-17 (NLT) to see what happened next:

But then David's conscience began bothering him because he had cut Saul's robe. ⁶*'The Lord knows I shouldn't have done that to my lord the king,' he said to his men. 'The Lord forbid that I should do this to my lord the king and attack the Lord's anointed one, for the Lord himself has chosen him.'* ⁷*So David restrained his men and did not let them kill Saul.*

After Saul had left the cave and gone on his way, ⁸*David came out and shouted after him, 'My lord the king!' And when Saul looked around, David bowed low before him.*

⁹*Then he shouted to Saul, 'Why do you listen to the people who say I am trying to harm you?* ¹⁰*This very day you can see with your own eyes it isn't true. For the Lord placed you at my mercy back there in the cave. Some of my men told me to kill you, but I spared you. For I said, 'I will never harm the king—he is the Lord's anointed one.'* ¹¹*Look, my father, at what I have in my hand. It is a piece of the hem of your robe! I cut it off, but I didn't kill you. This proves that I am not trying to harm you and that I have not sinned against you, even though you have been hunting for me to kill me.'*

¹²*'May the Lord judge between us. Perhaps the Lord will punish you for what you are trying to do to me, but I will never harm you.* ¹³*As that old proverb says, 'From evil people come evil deeds.' So you can be sure I will never harm you.* ¹⁴*Who is the king of Israel trying to catch anyway? Should he spend his time chasing one who is as worthless as a dead dog or a single flea?* ¹⁵*May the Lord therefore judge which of us is right and punish the guilty one. He is my advocate, and he will rescue me from your power!'*

¹⁶*When David had finished speaking, Saul called back, 'Is that really you, my son David?' Then he began to cry.* ¹⁷*And he said to David, 'You are a better man than I am, for you have repaid me good for evil.'*

Talk about a man who acted with integrity and respect for God and His timing. There is an old saying that goes, "Having the right thing at the wrong time is still the wrong thing!" How often do we take a situation that may "seem" right and try to make it work with all of our might only to find out it wasn't so "right" after all? It might be the wrong thing, or it may be the right thing at the wrong time. Trying to make it work at the wrong time will wear you out. Please believe me, I've tried it a few times . . . sadly.

It is important to notice that David actively served God while he waited to be crowned king of Israel. He was anointed to be king of Israel as a boy and yet in the meantime, he was a shepherd, messenger, musician, soldier, and a servant to the reigning King, Saul. All of these positions held some valuable experiences and training that David would need later on in his life.

The same is true for you. Please do not begrudge this time. It is necessary. Know this, dear sister, the training season does not mean the forgotten season. You may be out in the sheep fields right now, but take in the process and enjoy the time because God is anointing you for a powerful move into the palace.

The Lonely Times

Why do you say, O Jacob, and speak, O Israel: 'My way is hidden from the Lord, And my just claim is passed over by my God?' Have you not known? Have you not heard? The everlasting God, the LORD, the Creator of the ends of the earth, neither faints nor is weary. His understanding is unsearchable. He gives power to the weak, and to those who have no might He increases strength. Even the youths shall faint and be weary, and the young men shall utterly fall, But those who hope in the Lord shall renew their strength; They shall mount up with wings like eagles, They shall run and not be weary, They shall walk and not faint. (Isaiah 40:27-31 NKJV)

This was a passage of scripture on which I would lean heavily during the wait. I remember at times asking the questions: "Lord, where are you? I am still single. When will you move in this waiting?" Sure enough, when I went to the Lord with these inquiries, I would hear scriptures like these in Isaiah come to life in my mind causing my faith to soar.

In my prayer time, I would often sit with my journal in hand and ask the Lord if there was anything He wanted to say to me. In those moments, I would feel Him reassure me that He was actively preparing the way and that He was excited for the day when He would reveal what He had been working on all along. I found such encouragement through these precious encounters.

The Wait is valuable for many reasons. I love the verse in Deuteronomy 8:3 (NKJV) that talks about the Israelites wandering around in the desert before they entered the land that God had promised them. They kept complaining about their circumstances and in this passage, the Bible tells us the purpose for their wait: "So He humbled you, allowed you to hunger, and fed you with manna which you did not know nor did your fathers know, that He might make you know that man shall not live by bread alone; but man lives by every word that proceeds from the mouth of the LORD."

If we always got everything we wanted we'd be completely spoiled, wouldn't we? I would also venture to say that we would stop thinking that we even needed God—that we could take care of ourselves and plan our own futures for our own pleasure and self-glory. That just will not do for a God who desires to be in relationship with us. I believe that He allows us to hunger or *wait* so that we will always know that we cannot or would not want to live without Him.

You were made to soar far above the wind and waves.
Your heart was made to live in a place of true surrender
To be with Me far beyond your hopes and dreams
Your story will unfold as you wait for Me.

-Amber Gallagher, "Made to Soar," 2002

The Seemingly Forgotten Times

There is a powerful temptation to feel as if you are forgotten during this waiting period. The enemy will hurl his lies to drive this point home. He may even try to convince you that God is holding out on you, but that, dear friend is a lie. The enemy is speaking his native tongue. Do not give in to believing him. You are not forgotten. When it seems that nothing is going on, I guarantee you that events are in motion in the heavenly realm.

To be honest, in my own journey it did feel bittersweet, at times, to watch as others seemed to be receiving the very gifts that I desperately desired from the Lord—husbands, babies, and homes of their own. It was an especially keen experience when these people were those I had helped counsel and minister to throughout their junior high and high school days. When I would feel my heart want to go there, I would immediately start to pray God's blessing for them and God's comfort for me as I waited. Please don't get me wrong. It is exciting to watch good things happen to people and I am genuinely thrilled when a person's dreams come true, but there were days when I would feel an ache of sadness in my heart as well as moments when I would send up a cry, "Lord, You haven't forgotten me, right?"

I found some personal journal entries which were written during some of those hard times:

9/19/04 Amber age 26

Lord, I find myself longing for a family today. I want to have a home and children. Lord, I pray that you would speak to my husband on my behalf. Help me to 'be all here' right now. I know that you have a mission for me.

12/19/04

I held a baby tonight and I was reminded of Your promise to me. Lord, sometimes my arms and my heart ache to hold a child of my own.

Then, of course, I would often sense the Lord encouraging me:

9/26/08 Amber age 30

[I felt like the Lord said to me]:

'I have heard your prayers and I am answering you. Your husband will treasure you. You will be My gift to him. Your home will be filled with laughter and song. The aroma of praise coming up from your home will be a sweet-smelling savor to Me. I will take great delight in you and I will dwell with you and you will know My presence.'

On the other side of this particular waiting journey, as I look back, I am grateful to the Lord for His comfort along the way. He has done what He promised. God is the perfect Father who longs to give good gifts to His children. He knows the right time and situation to bring a promise to fruition. Believing without seeing (FAITH) is not always easy, but it is always blessed. Now that God has brought my husband into my life, I find myself extremely grateful and yet again in the place of trusting God's timing as I wait for other dreams to come. I am beginning to understand that the wait will forever be a part of this life's journey. Oh, I so want to do it well.

What Does a Lady Do During the Wait?

That's a great question. Did you know that God literally watches to "strengthen those whose hearts are fully committed to Him" (2 Chronicles 16:9). He's not giving you this strength so that you can lock yourself in your bedroom until He brings about your promises, hopes, and dreams. *Oh, please don't!* He wants you to be active during this time of waiting.

In the Bible, several Hebrew words are used for the word wait. One instance, *qavah* means *to wait, look eagerly for; to collect, bind together* (Isaiah 26:8, 40:31, 33:2, Psalm 52:9).[1] During your time of singleness, eagerly await and look for God's hand moving in your present circumstances. Gather up all of these experiences—every lesson, every blessing. They will be the foundation of your love affair with Christ and any ministry He calls you to throughout your entire life.

Another Hebrew word used for wait is *sharath*. This sense of wait means to *wait upon someone, to minister; serve, to be a servant* (Nehemiah 10:36, Deuteronomy 18:7).[2] This is not like waiting in line at the grocery store to check out, but more like the idea of a waiter or waitress actively serving others. You are able, during this time, to solely devote your life to the Lord, developing a love affair with Him without the added demands of serving a husband and children (1 Corinthians 7:33-35). It can be such a beautiful time of getting to know your Savior, if you'll let it. This relationship you build with Jesus will be what sustains you when you are running on fumes because you've chased a two-year-old around the house all day. When you come to a place where you find joy in serving others, it can be great preparation for the heart of service that you will naturally bring into your marriage and family. This heart will bless your future family and they will be able to thrive in this God-centered environment. May you enjoy this time and let it mold you and give you ability for the next chapter of your life at the same time.

The last Hebrew word I wanted to look at is the word *tsaphah*. It indicates wait in the form of *watching, observing like that of a watchman* (Psalm 5:3, Micah 7:7, Proverbs. 31:27).[3]

She carefully watches everything in her household and suffers nothing from laziness. (Proverbs 31:27 NLT)

Notice that this godly woman is not sitting on the couch watching TV or texting all day. She watches over her home and is not idle or lazy. She is productively active.

In spring 2008 I was still living with my parents when I felt the Lord speak to my heart: "Amber, I'm going to give you a home so that you can begin to learn the responsibilities of managing a household." You see, I had my eye on this little yellow cottage that had come up for sale across the street from my parents' house. We found out it was being foreclosed on and the bank wanted to sell it quickly and quite affordably for even my single girl's modest budget. I fell in love with it and began to pray for God's will. After a lengthy process, I was given the keys to my very own house! It was such a sweet time—certainly a lot of work, but I truly enjoyed it. At the time the Lord gave that house to me, I did not realize He was pulling the puzzle pieces of my story together. Little did I know that in October of 2010 I would be marrying my husband and we would end up living quite comfortably in this little cottage for the first few years as we saved and planned for our future. I look back on how all of that turned out and am struck again with the revelation that God is often working in ways that cannot be seen or understood in the moment. However, in the end, we will look back and know He was in control, providing for us every step of the way. After all, He knows what we will need before we ask or even realize we need to ask (Matthew 6:8).

What does a lady do during in the wait? If I may, I would like to share with you the following priorities that I believe the Lord asked me to actively spend time on before I got married:

1. Fall in love with your First Love.
2. Find the treasure in singleness.
3. Determine God's dreams for you.
4. Become the woman you long to be.
5. Be a part of your love story . . . long before your prince ever comes.

Perhaps He is asking the same of you?

7

Fall in Love with Your First Love

Our first priority should be to fall in love. I am talking about a full-scale love affair with Jesus, and in order for us to thrive; this must be an ever-growing relationship. Many would try and persuade you that having it "all" in life is about physical beauty, fame, wealth or romantic relationships. People clamor and fight to obtain these things, but are they fulfilled? Do they really have it "all" when they get it all? Think of the celebrities you watch that turn to drugs, alcohol or destructive relationships in order to numb their pain. I once heard a Johnny Cash song from late in his life and career called "Hurt." It's pretty telling as it sums up the kind of empire this world has to offer. What does all of the wealth and fame do for a person in the end?

> *What have I become my sweetest friend?*
> *Everyone I know goes away in the end.*
> *And you could have it all, my empire of dirt.*
> *I will let you down. I will make you hurt.*[1]

Even the great King Solomon of the Bible had every pleasure the world could possibly offer. He was undoubtedly the wisest and perhaps the richest man to ever live, yet in the end claimed that it was all "meaningless" and that the true purpose of a person's existence is to "fear (revere) God and obey His commands." (See Ecclesiastes 12:13, parenthesis added.)

'For in Him we live and move and have our being.' (Acts 17:28a NIV)

We were always meant to be with our Creator. A life lived without Him leaves us empty, void of the purpose for which we were even placed on this earth. We collect things only to see them for what they are—an empire of dirt. We will never escape this insatiable need to be with our God. He alone satisfies to the utmost.

We can develop and grow in our relationship with God by simply being with Him, including Him in our lives. This may happen through prayer, reading the Word, listening to Christian music, mediating on His goodness or fellowshipping with other believers. We have to make a concerted effort to establish these habits as priority in our lives. I heard Beth Moore once say that "in order to live the Christian life, you have to be deliberate about it." A close relationship with God does not happen by accident! Let's take time to pursue avenues in which we can actively grow our personal relationship with God.

Prayer

I was ashamed of myself for the audacity to lead Bible studies, evangelize, work for God daily, but spend no personal time with Him in prayer, in conversation or even in confession.

-Becky Tirabassi, *Let Prayer Change Your Life*[2]

A friend of mine had introduced me to a book, called *Let Prayer Change Your Life*, written by Becky Tirabassi. The above confession from Mrs. Tirabassi affected me pretty profoundly because it was the cry of my own heart. I was so overly busy doing *for* God that I wasn't spending much time *with* Him. I would end many days falling asleep on God as I lay in bed trying to pray or I'd rush by Him in the mornings throwing out a generic, "Thank you Lord for all your blessings." I knew that God deserved more than I was giving, but I didn't have the time to explore it and when I did sit down with Him, I was at a loss as to what to do when I got there. I was burned out and feeling drained when my friend recommended this book. I began to practice the discipline of setting this time aside with a method that proved exciting, rewarding, and productive. I began to actively hear from the Lord every day.

It was during a Morning Prayer time when the Lord spoke to me so urgently that I felt my heart pound in expectation. Something "important" was going to happen in this particular day. I was given direction to "watch for this moment" and that I would need to "speak the Lord's words."

Later that day, I was presenting to a group of young people on the topics of purity and abstinence when after class, a young lady approached me. This girl was pregnant with a second child and thinking of having an abortion this time around. She asked for my thoughts on the matter.

Immediately, my mind went on red alert, "Oh God, help me. What do I do?" We sat down together and she began to unravel her story. This young lady was afraid and did not want to go through the process of giving birth again. She felt alone and in turmoil. While she was talking, I felt the Lord nudge me and I knew that this was that "important" moment He had spoken of and prepared me for earlier that morning.

I didn't know what else to say except that the Lord had spoken to me about her during my prayer time that morning—that God cared about her. She was important to Him and so was this child she carried.

Tears streamed down her face as we talked about how precious life is and that God is the only One who creates life as we are knit together and given breath by Him in our mothers' wombs. Every child is reverently and wonderfully made by God (Psalm 139). This young lady walked away from the conversation with a much lighter countenance and said that she now "felt peace." Praise the Lord! What if I had not been with the Lord that morning or what if I had been too "busy" to hear from God about this beautiful young lady? She needed Him so desperately and so did I in order to meet head on with this life and death situation. This experience confirmed to me once again that spending time with the Lord had to be a priority. How could I claim that God was my Savior and Friend? How was He my Priority if I never took time to develop a deep relationship with Him?

The Power of Life and Death

In your pursuit of a consistent prayer life, I encourage you to find what works for you. You may like to journal your prayers and/or speak them aloud. I love to write down my prayers because it helps this scattered gal keep focused. I once heard Becky Tirabassi speak at a women's conference where she compared journaling our prayers to having "eye contact with God." Without our focused effort, we may be tempted to start dreaming about doing laundry, washing dishes or getting dinner started. I have also felt at times that praying aloud was vital for pushing back the enemy's charges against me. There is great power in speaking God's truth. Every time the enemy attacked Jesus, he responded by saying, "It is written." (See Matthew 4.) He spoke the Words of God and the enemy left Him. The Bible says that the "power of life and death is in your tongue" (Proverbs 18:21). We can literally speak prayer and blessing over our lives as well as the lives of our loved ones, by praying scripture and declaring aloud the promises of God. On the other hand, we also have the ability to tear someone apart with harsh and unfeeling words or talk ourselves into being overwhelmed with stress and depression if we consistently spew our negative comments.

Pray Without Ceasing

The Bible tells us to pray without ceasing (1 Thessalonians 5:17). This used to confuse me a little. How could I possibly pray all day long without ever stopping? I don't think the writer was saying that we are to pray out loud all day long because that is impossible in many of situations. I think he was encouraging us to include God in every part of our lives. We simply must make the decision to look for Him. It's actually pretty fun to notice a breathtaking sunset and offer up a simple "Thank You!" I always like to tell the Lord I think He is an amazing artist and I appreciate His masterpieces. Perhaps you could start in the morning by surrendering your day to Him, look for and acknowledge Him throughout the day, and lay your head down on the pillow at night talking over the day and thanking Him for what He has done. One thing is certain, to include God in your life is an ongoing endeavor—it never has to stop.

Get Together

Praying with others is powerful too. You may want to meet for a Bible study or call each week to pray over your concerns with a friend. The Bible is clear to say that when two people agree in God's name and ask God "according to His will," then it will be done (Matthew 18:19). I have a couple of people in my life that I know I could call if I am going through a difficult circumstance and cannot find the words to pray. They are faithful companions in this journey.

Confess your sins to each other and pray for each other so that you may be healed. The earnest prayer of a righteous person has great power and produces wonderful results. (James 5:16 NLT)

You may want to change it up a bit. I have personally preferred all of these methods for various situations and I have also found that different seasons of my life have determined the different methods that I have used. The important part of prayer is to keep striving to make it happen often. Many nights, I will have to look at my calendar to see when I can schedule my time with God for the following day. At times, it will be in the morning, on my lunch break or after work. I will even make plans to arrive at a particular meeting early in order to sit in my car and pray or read my Bible. Making appointments with God is well worth the time and effort. We wouldn't blow off a breakfast meeting with a friend. How much more courtesy should we show the Ancient of Days? My friend, the simple truth is that we cannot survive without communing with God. He is the One who keeps us pure, steady, confident, and on the right track.

The Word

There are many ways to study the Word of God. You may want to read the Bible through in a year. There are Bibles that are broken down with a daily reading or perhaps you might prefer an online reading plan. Another idea could be to study a particular subject or Biblical figure. I personally like to do Bible studies on different topics written by Beth Moore, Joyce Meyer, Lisa Turkhurst, and Nancy Lee Demoss. Make sure that the authors you select are those that you trust spiritually. Another option would be to venture on your own and study a topic or passage by reading it, looking up commentary (explanation and interpretation) on the passage, and then searching the Hebrew meanings of words in the chapters you are studying. I would definitely recommend that you write down anything you discover in your studies. This can be such an exciting journey for you. The more you dig into the Word, the more you learn about your Savior who is worth the time and effort. Also, keep in mind that the more you read the Bible, the more you will crave to find out what God's Word has to say to you. There is immense treasure within its pages. You can't afford to miss it.

Mentors and Friendships

The online dictionary.com describes a mentor as a *wise and trusted counselor*.[3]

I can't say enough about mentors and how important and necessary their godly wisdom and counsel is for our lives. The Lord has ordained these special relationships to help us grow into noble women of godly character.

These older women must train the younger women to love their husbands and their children, ⁵to live wisely and be pure, to work in their homes, to do good, and to be submissive to their husbands. Then they will not bring shame on the word of God. (Titus 2:4-5 NLT)

    I would encourage you to pray and ask the Lord to show you who would be a beneficial mentor for you. Perhaps a woman who has been able to make it through similar struggles as you. She can share with you wisdom from her journey that may serve to spare you from unnecessary detours.

    I have found mentors in lots of different places. Many have come to me in the form of authors whose books I have read or speakers at certain conferences. I have typically found that different women have various gifts from which I can pattern. For instance, one woman in my life is gifted at showing hospitality. When you go to her home, you definitely walk away feeling loved and appreciated. Another friend is wise and knowledgeable in understanding scriptures and how they relate to our lives. I will often go to her with spiritual questions and for advice and prayer. Another has the gift of organization. I love to check out her pantry—and she lets me. I love to glean from her creative organization ideas. There is another lady who is artistic and always has great ideas on how to bless others through gifts or acts of service. When you start looking, you will often find the people around you to be absolute treasures in your life. Learn from them. If you struggle to find these people, for the time being, check out a few trusted Christian authors, do an online study or sign up for a conference in your area.

The Inner Circle

Do not be misled: Bad company corrupts good character. (1 Corinthians 15:33 NIV 1984)

It is vital to surround yourself with friends who are in love with Jesus. They should be people who will help encourage you in the ways of God, rising above the standards of this world. They can remind you of God's promises and pray for you when you are struggling. In order to connect on a deep level, your friends need to be able to share in the most important part of your life—your relationship with God.

If you'll notice, in the life of Jesus, he spoke and ministered to everyone. He traveled with a ministry team of twelve, and He had three that were in His inner circle (Matthew 26:37). These three were the ones who went into the deepest places with him.

We are called to be kind, thoughtful, and generous—to minister to those around us. However, there are probably a few who we would consider to be our core friends and confidants. In my life, I have a handful of friends with whom I can learn in the Lord together by doing Bible studies, weekend ladies' retreats or simply getting together to talk about what the Lord is doing in our lives. We constantly lift one another up in prayer.

These are ladies that I affectionately refer to as, "Women of the Round Table," a named coined by dear prayer warriors as we would gather weekly around the kitchen table. Oh what trials we conquered using our double-edged swords as they lay opened before us guiding us as we wrestled through our circumstances.

In Matthew 7:6, the Bible cautions to be careful not to "cast your pearls" or expose your deepest heart issues before inappropriate listeners unless of course the Lord leads you otherwise. In a world of imperfect people, some will be tempted to become jealous of what the Lord has promised you and even scoff at your so-called "naivety."

Oftentimes, you will be able to share your testimony after the breakthrough or promise is fulfilled. Perhaps the prayer and details through the trial are between you, the Lord, and your inner circle.

It is a wise woman who will take the necessary time to determine who the inner circle members should be. There may only be a few, but you will be glad once you see what a blessing it is to have such sisters in the Lord.

Joseph's Dream

Think of the young man Joseph's story in the Bible. The Lord gave him dreams depicting a time when he would be in a position of authority over his own brothers and they would one day bow down to him. When the brothers heard of his dreams, they were angry and therefore plotted to kill Joseph. He ended up being thrown into a pit and in an unexpected turn was sold into slavery. It all came full circle when years later, Joseph became the second in command of all Egypt, which was the only country at the time with an abundance of food in the face of a devastating famine. The brothers found themselves on their knees in front of Joseph, pleading not only for bread, but for their lives to be spared. Joseph reveals himself to the brothers and they are overcome as they realize that Joseph's dreams from long ago had in fact come to pass. (See Genesis 37.)

Hannah

Still other well-meaning bystanders may even try to talk you out of a promise you believe is from God. Not everyone will have the same excitement and drive for your dreams and promises as you may. In fact, your quest for God's supernatural and miraculous power to be unleashed in your life may be quite uncomfortable to some as in the case of a dear young lady in my life named Hannah. As I write this, it has been two weeks since Hannah was in a severe car accident. Her neck was broken and her spine crushed. The doctors have told her that she has a zero to one percent chance of walking again. Yet, she believes God is going to work a miracle and we are standing with her in belief. There are skeptics, but they cannot deny that her faith is something to cause the most cynical to marvel. I look forward to see how God will move for dear Hannah. The last word I received was two days ago. Hannah has been able to move her feet and has felt sensations in her knees and recently in her upper legs. Oh, Jesus!

The Church

Many see the church as the building in which we gather to sing worship sets and listen to sermons. However, the True Church is the body of Believers. This community is so essential in our spiritual walk that the Bible instructs us not to "forsake the assembling of ourselves together" (Hebrews 10:25). We all need encouragement and prayer. We were made to be in relationship with God as well as with our brothers and sisters in Christ. There is something powerful, satisfying, and peaceful about gathering with those who have the same heart to worship, adore, know, and serve God. There is an unmistakable feeling of home.

A friend of mine went through two miscarriages. She told me how grateful she was that her church family had gathered around her in those times. It brought such comfort to her and to her family. A genuine family of believers will be there for you and will hold your arms up when you are tired. They will invest in your life by seeking to know you and allowing themselves to be known by you.

In addition to seeing church as part of our family, my husband and I like to think of spending time at church as a kind of filling station. We pour out love, compassion, and energy throughout the week and then we come back to church for refreshment to turn around and be poured out again.

"Do Not Forget Your First Love."

Time and again I have felt the Lord say to me, "Amber, do not forget your First Love." As with any relationship, in order to keep a thriving union with Christ, we must continue to pursue Him and watch for Him as He constantly works to woo us. My husband and I like to keep things in our relationship exciting. We love to change it up and find different ways to have fun and grow together whether that is through horseback riding, talking over dinners, visiting parks and historical sites or ministering together. If we were to ever stop pursuing one another or spending time together, our relationship would be in trouble. I believe that the same is true in our relationship with our First Love, God. We pursue Him by spending time with Him in prayer, studying the Bible, fellowshipping with other believers, learning from godly friends and mentors, singing, serving others, and sharing the gospel of Jesus Christ. Every one of these activities can be an act of our worship that draws us deeper into this romance with the One True God.

8

Find the Treasure in Singleness

A woman who is no longer married or has never been married can be devoted to the Lord and holy in body and in spirit. But a married woman has to think about her earthly responsibilities and how to please her husband. (1 Corinthians 7:34b NLT)

When people, most of whom were married, quoted this scripture to me, it would always cause me to wince a little. In my immaturity, I would want to remind them, "But *you're* married!"

Obviously this verse is true. I learned a valuable lesson when I realized that the single season was a gift. One I can wish away or waste, but a gift nevertheless. When I was single, it *was* true that I had more time for devotions, ministries, and mission trips. The Lord had my undivided attention, passion, and energy. This was a beautiful time with Him once I let it be. During this chapter in my life that I now look back at fondly, God taught me to soak in His presence. His voice became more recognizable as I captured His Words in my personal journals which are filled with scriptures detailing His promises for my future as well as my present. God was the One I went to about paying bills when the money was scarce, making final decisions when I was unsure which way to go, and sharing dreams that felt too precious to be voiced to others. I began to know Him as my Confidant and my Provider. I needed that time to get to know Him.

I have come to look at my marriage and the prospect of being a mother, not as relationships to fulfill or complete me—God already did that—but I view them as my own little mission field. Right now, my most important ministry is to support, honor, cherish, and encourage my husband.

Looking at 1 Corinthians 7:34 in this light has really helped me to understand that this verse is not a rationalization for not being married, but more than that, this scripture is a call for women to find joy, wisdom, and treasure during this sacred alone time with our Creator. There are many married women who have known the regret of not valuing this gift that was meant to be theirs for a time. The greatest Husband we will ever know takes the initiative to devote Himself to us and we are undistracted in our ability to give our whole heart back to Him. He comes to complete us so that we will always know where our joy and satisfaction comes from—not our earthly relationships, but from God alone.

The single years can also be a time for establishing habits of prayer and reading the Bible, which will in turn be with us throughout our entire lives.

I wrote the following entry in my journal while still single:

I love to sneak out in the cool of the day and walk or sit with the Lord. I have come to cherish these times and I will guard them when I am married and have children because I know how important they are to my spirit woman. I cannot live without my time with Him and I now know that.

Ministry Opportunities

And He told them, 'Go into all the world and preach the Good News to everyone.' (Mark 16:15 NLT)

Now is a great time to experience many different types of ministry whether it is for youth, children, nursing homes, camps, outreaches, singing groups or mission trips. There is a plethora of possibilities.

Taking mission trips is one really great use of time right now. I have had friends who have traveled for months or years at a time to Ukraine, Africa, Taiwan, and Honduras.

Once, our youth group took a trip to minister alongside our church's missionary, who was stationed in Belgium, France, and England. We facilitated youth conferences and summer camps. It was a beautiful experience. My fellow travelers and I walked away with an appreciation for the freedoms that we had back home and a love for the people of a completely different culture. It was a truly rewarding and satisfying experience because we are made to serve and to pour out our lives for others. There is no greater feeling in the world than to feel God smiling down on you for loving the people that He deeply loves—those who are down and out, broken, and hurting. I am a firm believer that everyone should involve themselves in mission work if at all possible. It seems that even getting out of our normal culture and comfort zone produces a deepened love for God and an escape from our human tendency to be self-focused.

Opportunities not always available or appropriate during the season of marriage and family abound in single life. This doesn't mean that once you are married with children that you cannot go on mission trips or be involved in different ministries. I am simply reiterating that singleness will be a time to experience things that the demands of managing a home or tending to spouse and parental responsibilities cannot always allow for.

Serving Christ

For everything there is a season, a time for every activity under heaven. (Ecclesiastes 3:11 NLT)

I have found this scripture to be a powerful way to look at life. Nothing in this life lasts forever. It's all for an "appointed time"— jobs, schooling, ministries, relationships, and singleness. Instead of wishing the time away, what if we would be determined to live each of these seasons to the fullest, which will bring true joy and contentment?

The following is an excerpt I wrote for this chapter while still single:

In my heart, I feel that there will be a different type of ministry that I will be involved in than what I am doing now. If that is where I was focused, I would miss so much of the wonderful opportunity that is here now. I want so much to be married and have children, but right now, I have more time for other ministries.

Ruth

One of my favorite Biblical characters to study is Ruth. She is a woman of great integrity from a town called Moab. She married into an Israelite family and when her husband, brother-in-law, and father-in-law die, she chooses to stay with her mother-in-law, Naomi, whom she dearly loves. After these tragedies, when Naomi decides to return to her hometown, Bethlehem, Ruth pleads to go with her.

In Bethlehem, Ruth provides for herself and Naomi by picking up wheat left behind for the poor in the fields of the wealthy landowners. She ends up gleaning on the land belonging to a man named Boaz. He notices Ruth and greatly esteems her after hearing how she left her home country to come and support Naomi. He treats Ruth kindly by offering her protection and generously providing her extra portions of grain. Finally, Ruth lets him know that she is in fact interested in him too, at which time he sets out to make her his bride.

In the end, Boaz and Ruth are married and both Naomi and Ruth will be taken care of and loved for the rest of their lives. It is also important to note that Ruth is the grandmother of King David and in the family line of Jesus Christ. What a turnaround from loss and heartache to joy and honor. God has a way of doing that. It was God's plan to "prosper and not harm" (Jeremiah 29:11) Ruth from the beginning!

Ruth was a single woman who during her singleness decided to serve someone else instead of focusing on her own relationship status. In doing so, the whole town heard about her goodness to Naomi and they all spoke highly of her . . . in the ear of Boaz (Ruth 2:6, 11, 3:11). As a man of integrity himself, He was drawn to her servant-hearted devotion.

Ladies, we have got to stop complaining about what we don't have, focus on serving others, and let God get in the ear of that future husband. Dear sister, with God speaking highly of you to others, you cannot miss out on His best for you. Ruth could've gotten bitter or angry and blamed God for her singleness. She could have decided to take matters into her own hands and find herself a husband by chasing men and being consumed with relationship after relationship, but instead she showed kindness, goodness, servanthood, and humility, and God took care of ALL her needs.

Building Relationships

Our single years provide great opportunities to focus on the relationships that we do have at the moment. We have time to be with our parents, brothers, sisters, nieces, and nephews. I decided to spend quality time with my niece and nephews (great preparation for being a parent). I would on occasion show up at their house with ice cream, pick them up after school and take them out to eat or we'd visit our local park, which housed this magnificent castle playground. I'm not sure who had more fun, the kids or me. I wanted to pour into their lives and let them know that they are loved not only by me but by the Lord. I cherish those times. My niece still runs to me every time she sees me. There is nothing like that kind of greeting. This investment in their lives has afforded many opportunities to speak truth into their little minds and hearts. What a privilege.

During these single years, I also loved the free time to develop godly friendships that have brought me years of joy and support. We have ministered together, prayed together, and had crazy fun together. We would and still do plan what we affectionately call, "Girl's Night." These special nights may involve dinners, trips to the ice cream or tea parlor, Christmas parties or perhaps Jane Austen move nights, all of which are coupled with lots of intriguing conversation. What great fun to develop deep relationships with such beautiful women of God.

When you and I take our focus off our expectations of what we think we need and want at any specific time, then the waiting gets a lot easier. There is such a peace when we trust that God will take care of our needs. He will do it very well indeed. Meanwhile, we can enjoy our time pursuing the treasures of friends and family, ministry opportunities, and developing healthy spiritual habits in our personal time with God. You can be sure that in the meantime, God is busy working out His perfect plan for your life. He is an Adventurer and I promise He will thrill you in every season of your life. You won't want to miss a moment of it.

But seek first the kingdom of God and His righteousness, and all these things shall be added to you. (Matthew 6:33 NKJV)

Determine God's Dreams for You

'For I know the plans I have for you,' declares the LORD, 'plans to prosper you and not to harm you, plans to give you hope and a future.' (Jeremiah 29:11 NIV)

Since my parents were in full-time ministry during most of my child and early adulthood, my upbringing was saturated in the church world. I am grateful to my parents that there has never been a time when I did not know the name of Jesus and that He "loves me this I know for the Bible tells me so."

I first felt the call to work in ministry around the age of sixteen. Before that time, I had plans to enjoy my future career as an equestrian veterinarian. After I realized that perhaps God wanted me to work directly in a ministry capacity, I assumed that I would be a missionary or pastor's wife because at that time I didn't know a lot of women in ministry other than in those roles. It was a journey to get from there to the ministry that I believe God has laid before me today. On my path to discovery, I have been privileged to take part in a variety of worthwhile ventures that served to expose me to all sorts of different ministry situations. These opportunities ranged from being a youth leader, worship director, conference speaker, Sunday school and Wednesday school teacher, and Director of Positive Life

Choices at The Community Pregnancy Center. I have also been fortunate to sing in a couple of bands, in our church choir, and at youth conferences. I am grateful and certainly cherish all of these opportunities the Lord used in my life to build the spiritual muscles of endurance, self-discipline, and leadership. Every one has been instrumental in shaping who I am as a woman, a Christian, and a speaker/author.

I yearned to serve the Lord and because I could never put my finger on what it was that I was supposed to do for God, I would at times find myself getting anxious. I cannot tell you how often I came to the Lord, praying for Him to make His will for me clear. It was on my lips every day and I would feel distraught at the thought of missing a cue or word of direction from Him. I would pray, "Lord, I don't want to miss it; please help me not to miss You."

One day, in prayer, I felt Him quietly impress upon my heart, "My will is a lot harder to miss out on than you think."

"What do you mean?" I replied.

He went on to say, "Amber, if you get up every day and keep your eyes on Me; If you ask Me to lead you each day, I will. As you follow, it will result in an entire lifetime of living out My perfect will for you."

You see, I kept waiting for God to drop into my heart some big amazing, world-changing idea. He was interested in my daily surrender to Him and in doing so, I could change the world around me. God has allowed me to embark on some thrilling adventures, but all of it has happened through my daily relationship with Him. As He has opened one door after another, I have simply walked through them.

You are not going to miss out on God's will for your life if you commit to walk with Him daily. He will lead you into any and everything He has designed for you. First comes relationship, then vision. He wants more than anything, I think, to be known by you. Seek Him and He'll add all the things to your life that He wants to. (See Matthew 6:33.) Be determined to cherish every day of it!

Let's take a look at steps you may want to pursue as you are trying to determine God's dreams for you.

Ask the Lord

You do not have because you do not ask God. (James 4:2b NIV 1984)

I encourage you to ask the Lord to show you His will and plan for your life. He does not want you to live in confusion about this. Remember, He is interested in you serving Him even MORE than you are interested in it. Simply ask Him. Then listen and watch for Him to respond. We will cover the topic of Hearing God's Voice in a later chapter, but for now this simple truth is worth mentioning. He is a God who answers us when we call.

In the day of my trouble I will call to You: for You will answer me. (Psalm 86:7 NIV)

Write It Down

Then the LORD answered me and said: 'Write the vision and make it plain on tablets.' (Habakkuk 2:2a NKJV)

One great benefit of journaling your thoughts and prayers is that when you sense an idea, you can get it on paper immediately. Then, look for God to confirm or to keep speaking to you about this idea in His Word. In addition, He may use your pastor's sermons, Bible studies, and godly counsel from trusted mentors. Often, when I have written down an idea, it will start to constantly invade my thoughts. I begin to develop an excitement, passion, and assurance that God is moving. When the door opens to fulfill this mission, I know that it is Him. I have found that when the labor of love begins, the birth of the idea is certain.

Move in Faith

The priests will carry the Ark of the LORD, the Lord of all the earth. As soon as their feet touch the water, the flow of water will be cut off upstream, and the river will stand up like a wall. (Joshua 3:13 NLT)

The Lord asked me to resign from a position that I held for years. I had felt a growing dissatisfaction with this comfortable sameness. I would daydream about speaking and writing, but leaving meant changing the life that I had known for so long. Resigning leadership was hard, but I knew that the Lord had confirmed this decision many times. On my last day in this leadership position, I came home and the Lord began to speak to me of ideas that I had been contemplating for a while. From that moment on, the Lord led me to write and publish two Bible studies, start a ministry, and develop an ongoing event and speaking ministry.

I look back and realize how necessary it was to resign the position I had held previously in order to be free to pursue this personal life ministry. Now, instead of daydreaming, I am able to set a goal and spend the appropriate time to accomplish it.

The decision to make this move reminded me of a particular scene in the film "Indiana Jones: The Last Crusade." Mr. Jones is on an expedition to find the Holy Grail (cup) of Christ, which was believed to be used in "the last supper" with His disciples. Mr. Jones comes to a dramatic impasse. As the scene plays out, we see him standing on one side of a cavern cliff where the way forward is through an opening on the other side of a seemingly bottomless pit. It is only when he takes a leap of faith that he steps out onto a bridge that had existed all along but had been concealed as it blended into the cave surroundings.

There will be times you may have to leap, uncertain of where you will step down. Rest assured, if God is calling you to move, He has already prepared the bridge for you or perhaps your way will emerge like waters being parted allowing you to walk across your impasse on dry and solid ground.

Do It!

Why do you call me 'Lord, Lord,' and do not do what I say? I will show you what it's like when someone comes to me, listens to my teaching, and then follows it. ⁴⁸*It is like a person building a house who digs deep and lays the foundation on solid rock. When the floodwaters rise and break against that house, it stands firm because it is well built.* ⁴⁹*But anyone who hears and doesn't obey is like a person who builds a house without a foundation. When the floods sweep down against that house, it will collapse into a heap of ruins.* (Luke 6:46-49 NLT)

If you feel God calling you to act, the greatest thing you can do is obey. Obedience is extremely valuable to God and it is the key that will unlock unfathomable doors. We can daydream and plan, but we must be willing to step out and do the thing. Do it afraid if you must, but do it. Before getting the job, we must go to the interview. Before publishing the book, we must take the time to sit down and write it. Before marrying the husband, we must open ourselves up to love.

The Desires of Your Heart

Delight yourself in the LORD and he will give you the desires of your heart. (Psalm 37:4 NIV 1984)

Direct me in the path of your commands, for there I find delight. (Psalm 119:35 NIV 1984)

When we "delight in the Lord," He will give us the "desires of our heart." I used to think this meant that if I walked with the Lord, He would make *my dreams* come true. I have since understood this verse to mean that when I walk with God, He will place *His desires* inside of me.

In my personal walk, as previously mentioned, I have found that God's desires for me usually start as an idea and as the idea takes root in my heart, it becomes a full-fledged dream that I am desperate to passionately pursue. As I continue to pray about the desire and ask for guidance, the path to accomplish it becomes more clear. The excitement builds as I take steps to complete it and in the end, the idea brings glory to God and delight to my heart.

This was true when God nudged me to write a Bible study called, *The Princess Within: Living Like a Princess from the Inside Out*. At first it was an idea. The more I thought about it (which was often), the more I began to develop a passion and energy to see it completed. Once the study was printed, it was one of the most exhilarating sights to see. There are days that I look back in wonder at the absolute miracle of how that dream came together.

Once, the Lord even told me that accomplishing my dreams was a big part of the love story He was writing for my life. At first, I didn't quite understand, but then I thought about the people I knew who were already married with families. A few would comment about how they wished they would have traveled or finished college or had precious time during their single years to devote themselves to following the Lord with undistracted devotion. I do not think these individuals wished that they could get out of their marriages or current lives; it simply seems that perhaps they look back with a twinge of regret when they think about lost or wasted opportunities of which they did not take advantage. In this way, I think these regrets can hinder the enjoyment of their current blessings. For those of us who were single for many years, we are tempted to look at married individuals as having it all—the life we desire to have and yet some of these married people would love to have a chance to enjoy opportunities God is giving you right now such as finishing school, traveling or following other dreams.

Wherever you are, be all there. Live to the hilt every situation you believe to be the will of God.

-Jim Elliot, *The Journals of Jim Elliot*[1]

Seize the Day! -Horace, *Latin Poem*

So be careful how you live. Don't live like fools, but like those who are wise. [16] *Make the most of every opportunity in these evil days.* (Ephesians 5:15-16 NLT)

If we delight in the Lord and continue to grow closer to Him, the desires of our heart will actually be to carry out His desire for our life. All the good ideas, talent, and imagination come from Him.

Let's take a moment to clarify what you believe your God-given dreams to be. Keep in mind that His dreams in your life might not always seem overtly religious.

My Dreams

Make a list of dreams. Next to that dream, write out what it would take to accomplish it.

Dreams	**What will it take?**
(Ex. Travel to Paris, France)	(Flight, hotel, etc. Cost: $3,500)
_____	_____
_____	_____
_____	_____
_____	_____
_____	_____
_____	_____

Remember that your life will consist of many chapters. There is a time to be single, married, parenting, working, attending school, traveling, etc. and God's plans for you can be found in every one of these opportunities.

When I am doing a presentation for students, I love to ask them, "When do you start working to make your dreams come true?"

They will tell me, "When I get to college," or "When I'm 25."

Finally, one of them will come up with the answer, "Right now, Ms. Amber!"

Yes! Now is the time. Good habits, honorable character, fulfilled dreams, and healthy marriages don't simply appear. Each one of these accomplishments begins long before the dream is ever realized.

Marriage and Parenting 101

One theme that I would sense strongly during my time of singleness was the need for preparation. I am amazed at the lack of preparation most will undergo while they dream of marriage and parenting. A handful of couples will perhaps meet with a pastor maybe six or seven times before marrying, if that. For parental training, expectant parents may go through a Lamaze class, which basically focuses on breathing and the birth of your child, but what happens after that? Where can a girl enroll for a Marriage and Parenting class?

For any other life career, we would spend countless hours talking to counselors, job shadowing, and looking at colleges that would offer the best training program for our desired occupation. We would spend thousands upon thousands of dollars attending a university and possibly be there four years to almost a decade, depending on the field of interest. Then, we would have to take required tests to get from one phase of study to the other, probably interning often along the way.

It only makes sense to go through appropriate training in order to be successful at something, right? So, couldn't the same be said for the necessity of training before we become wives and mothers? Wouldn't it only make sense to use part of this waiting time to put ourselves through **marriage** and **parenting school**, so to speak?

If you want to be a good spouse, then start by learning to be a good daughter, sister, and friend to others. These are precious people

God has given us with whom we can practice healthy communication and servant-hearted humility. I was talking with my husband the other day about how I love being his friend. Truly great marriages are made of two people who can be great friends. They don't merely love each other, but they like each other too.

I would, and still do, love to sit down with women who have good healthy marriages. They've been doing this for thirty, forty, even fifty years and have a lot of experience to show for it. I like to interview them with questions like: "What are the things that you believe contribute to your successes and failures in marriage? What truths do you wish you had known before getting married?" I would also love to talk to newlyweds: "What are joys and struggles you are experiencing now at the start of your marriage? Are things as you expected? What has been unexpected? What are adjustments you have had to make already?"

You could plan time to spend in the homes of women who have a passion for training younger women in the faith. Perhaps you could take the time to learn from a woman who has an effective and loving parenting style. Ask her if you could observe a typical day in her home. What techniques has she found to be effective? Typically, when an individual has found a tactic or method that works, they are quite willing and even excited to share it with others. Please don't be afraid to ask.

I would encourage you to develop a healthy love of reading. When people tell me they don't like to read, it makes me a little sad. "How much you miss out on," I will respond. My sister-in-law, Tracy, likes to say that "God had His Word written down for us, so that must mean we are supposed to read!"

These days you can glean a lot of information from reading books about relationships, marriage, and parenting. It's like taking a college course from experts in the field, only much cheaper.

You may want to keep a separate notebook for each topic (i.e., marriage and parenting). Write down what you determine to be useful information. That way, when the time comes for marriage and family, you will have done the homework and you can brush up on any key findings that you want to put into practice. One important thing to remember is to NEVER STOP LEARNING. None of us will have ever "arrived," but we can certainly continue to become more and more accomplished.

We are responsible to take the opportunities we are given. There are lots of ways to practice for having your own household someday. We can develop responsible behaviors by cleaning, doing laundry or taking out trash. Be a productive member of your family right now. I encourage you to take advantage of the training ground before you and of course, we certainly want to daily rely on the Lord for guidance and wisdom. He is prepared for any and every circumstance that we would face. He knows how to guide every step of our uncertain way as we endeavor to follow His dreams for us.

Searching for Happily-Ever-After

I thought it would be fun to share with you some of my adventures in travel . . .

Mom and I in Chicago

Auschwitz Camp in Poland

The London Bridge

Jane Austen Center in Bath, England

Searching for Happily-Ever-After

Globe Theatre in London

Green Gables in Prince Edward Island, Canada

AMBER GALLAGHER

The Eiffel Tower in Paris, France

This is where I liked to spend a majority of my free time.

10

Become the Woman You Long to Be

A preacher told the story of a young college student. One weekend, instead of partying with her crowd as was usual, she came home to visit her parents. Sitting at the kitchen table with her mother she mused, "Mom, when will I find the kind of man to love me, who will be faithful and true, hard-working and responsible—a man of integrity who will have eyes only for me?"

Her mother paused and replied softly, "That type of man is not looking for a girl like you. A guy like that will be looking for a girl who has qualities similar to his." Ouch! The truth can certainly be painful. Nevertheless, this wise mother spoke what she knew she must.

What type of woman do you long to be? Do you want to be a woman after God's own heart? Now is the time to focus on becoming that noble woman of character. Instead of living aimlessly, you can consistently work to become an accomplished woman marked by her commitment to God.

I tell my students all the time, "You will attract the type of person that you are." I wanted to learn to be that woman of noble character, not only to be prepared for my future husband, but more importantly because that is how it should be with a daughter of The Great King. In my search I found that the Bible contains beautiful examples of this type of woman for a lady-in-waiting to emulate.

Helpful guidelines for godly living can be found in Galatians 5:19-26 and Proverbs 31:10-31.

The Fruit of the Spirit

When you follow the desires of your sinful nature, the results are very clear: sexual immorality, impurity, lustful pleasures, idolatry, sorcery, hostility, quarreling, jealousy, outbursts of anger, selfish ambition, dissension, division, envy, drunkenness, wild parties, and other sins like these. Let me tell you again, as I have before, that anyone living that sort of life will not inherit the Kingdom of God.

But the Holy Spirit produces this kind of fruit in our lives: love, joy, peace, patience, kindness, goodness, faithfulness, gentleness, and self-control. There is no law against these things!

Those who belong to Christ Jesus have nailed the passions and desires of their sinful nature to his cross and crucified them there. Since we are living by the Spirit, let us follow the Spirit's leading in every part of our lives. Let us not become conceited, or provoke one another, or be jealous of one another. (Galatians 5:19-26 NLT)

The Bible says that the Holy Spirit produces fruit in us. Have you ever met a couple who has been married for a really long time and found that this couple looks and acts like each other? Have you even found it true in your friendships that the more you hang out with your best friend, the more people comment on your similar mannerisms? You "rub off" on each other. The same is true with God. He is the epitome of love, joy, peace, patience, kindness, goodness, faithfulness, gentleness, and self-control. You will begin to act more like God the more you know and spend time with His Holy Spirit, who lives in you if you have accepted Christ as your Savior. The Bible also says that we can ask for the Holy Spirit to fill up our lives (Luke 11:13).

A friend of mine, David Mahan, always says, "Practice makes permanent." The more you spend time with God and practice portraying His qualities, the more second nature they will become for you.

The Proverbs 31 Woman of Virtue

Who can find a virtuous and capable wife? She is more precious than rubies. Her husband can trust her, and she will greatly enrich his life. She brings him good, not harm, all the days of her life. She finds wool and flax and busily spins it. She is like a merchant's ship, bringing her food from afar. She gets up before dawn to prepare breakfast for her household and plan the day's work for her servant girls. She goes to inspect a field and buys it; with her earnings she plants a vineyard. She is energetic and strong, a hard worker. She makes sure her dealings are profitable; her lamp burns late into the night.

Her hands are busy spinning thread, her fingers twisting fiber. She extends a helping hand to the poor and opens her arms to the needy. She has no fear of winter for her household, for everyone has warm clothes. She makes her own bedspreads. She dresses in fine linen and purple gowns. Her husband is well known at the city gates, where he sits with the other civic leaders. She makes belted linen garments and sashes to sell to the merchants.

She is clothed with strength and dignity, and she laughs without fear of the future. When she speaks, her words are wise, and she gives instructions with kindness. She carefully watches everything in her household and suffers nothing from laziness. Her children stand and bless her. Her husband praises her; 'There are many virtuous and capable women in the world, but you surpass them all!' Charm is deceptive and beauty does not last; but a woman who fears the LORD will be greatly praised. Reward her for all she has done. Let her deeds publicly declare her praise. (Proverbs 31: 10-31 NLT)

What instruction and treasure are found in these verses of the Proverbs 31 Woman of Virtue! This is truly a woman of godly character who works diligently to take care of her husband and family. She is creative and productive with her time—always kind and willing to help those in need while clothing herself with dignity and purity. This virtuous woman doesn't worry or complain about the future because she knows that she is in the Lord's hands. She respects and honors her husband and he can't help but speak highly of her. She also does him good ALL the days of her life. I was fortunate that one of my first projects when I took my position at the Community Pregnancy Center was to plan an event with beloved speakers/authors Eric and Leslie Ludy. I remember sitting under Leslie's teaching when she pointed out that ALL the days of a girl's life, as this scripture refers to, do not simply begin on her wedding day, but instead on the day she is created. What a concept—it means that we, just as this Proverbs 31 Woman of Virtue, are to honor our husband even *before* we know him and long before we are ever married.

The honest truth is that many women spend more time preparing for the actual wedding ceremony than they ever spend on becoming the type of godly woman who will graciously keep the vows and promises she is making on that day.

Isn't that amazing? When you become a godly woman, you are preparing yourself to be a good wife and mother. When you clothe yourself in dignity and modesty and your life is marked by purity and abstinence until marriage, you are doing a great honor to your husband long before he ever moves onto the scene. In doing so, people will notice that your life is different and they will respect you for it. You never know, one of those people in the crowd who take notice may actually be your future husband.

I once heard Beth Moore say, "When people ask what they can pray for me about, I always tell them, 'Please pray that I will love God.'" Your beauty, character, and integrity as a woman will all hinge on the proportion with which you love and commit your life to God and His divine role for you as His daughter. Everything in your life will be tied to this redeeming purpose and will ultimately serve to leave a legacy for others to follow just as the woman in Proverbs has done for us.

A Legacy Kind of Life

A good name is more desirable than great riches; to be esteemed is better than silver or gold. (Proverbs 22:1 NIV)

Ah! What's in a name? What's in a legacy? What *is* a legacy, you may ask? Well, simply put, it is what you leave behind. When your name is mentioned, it is how an individual may sum up the imprint you have made on their lives. What did you teach them? What did you show them about God? It is the Great Legacy Love Affair at work in your life. The legacy kind of life is such a real and breathtaking life that when people come in contact with it, it leaves them changed forever. They can no longer go back to "life as usual." The longing for something extraordinary is etched in the deepest part of their souls and they start to become hungry for it.

As I write this section, my thoughts continue to turn toward my late mother-in-law, Rita Gallagher. Although, we only ever met once briefly, I feel as if I knew her. According to my father-in-law, we met after an event where I had sung. Even though I don't remember the encounter all those years ago, I am grateful that God allowed that divine meeting to take place. It makes me smile.

You see, Rita developed breast cancer and passed away on October 8, 2007. When my husband and I got engaged, almost everyone we told would gush over us: "Oh, Rita would be so proud!" or "God has answered Rita's prayers!"

Another beautiful gift that God gave to me was that while Rita was struggling with cancer, I happened to work with a couple of ladies who went to her church. They would come in each morning and during our devotion time, we would pray for Rita Gallagher and her family. We would ask for healing, strength, and comfort for all of them. I had no idea that in those times God was allowing me to join in prayer with my future family and my future husband. What a supernatural gift! The thoughtfulness of God in orchestrating it so that I could be near in spirit to my husband during his profound loss still brings me to tears.

When people talk about Mrs. Rita, they cannot help the tears that gather in their eyes as they honor her godly legacy of a life well lived. I understand she was one of most giving and lovely of woman and this character has trickled down into the lives of her children and grandchildren after her. A friend of mine will often talk about how Rita would never fail to share a warm hug and a genuine smile, going out of her way for a heartfelt greeting. Before Rita, the young lady confessed that she never really hugged people. That is not the case anymore. Her kindness caused people to want to be better versions of themselves. The story told to me that I think of most is the one my sisters-in-law have recounted to me about her last days. As she was slipping into eternity, my mother-in-law wanted the song "Moving with the Lamb" played over and again. The words are powerfully descriptive of not only her earthy life, but also the life she was looking forward to and would know a few short days later:

> *For I'm dressed in a holy robe of God I'm surrounded*
> *By the Host from Heaven's court and the King of Kings*
> *And I drink from the holy cup of God I'm surrounded*
> *I'm moving with the Lamb*[1]

What a beautiful song for her home going. After we leave this earth, Oh, I pray that we would leave such a godly legacy for those who come behind us to follow. May they know that we were surrounded by the Lamb and that we lived to drink from the holy cup of His presence. May people always remember that it was the love affair with The Great King that was the most breathtaking aspect of our life. It was always Him who was behind the smile, the song, and the story.

Searching for Happily-Ever-After

Wayne and Rita Gallagher

Friends, after this life is over we will get to stand in the heavenly realm, face to face with our beautiful Savior. In that moment, we will not be thinking about the clothes we wore, the houses we built, the cars we drove or the lunch table we sat at in high school. We will be longing to hear Him say as in Matthew 25:23, "Well done, good and faithful servant. Enter into the joy of your Lord, The Great King!" May this truly be what you are living for and the kind of woman that you long to be.

Please take a moment . . .

Lord, I need you. Please help me to love you more. Give me a hunger to spend time with you. Holy Spirit, increase your fruit in my life. Help me to grow in love, joy, peace, patience, kindness, goodness, faithfulness, gentleness, and self-control. I want to honor you and leave behind a godly legacy as the Proverbs 31 Woman of Virtue did. I want to fulfill the purposes that You have ordained for my life before the world was created. Help me to grow to be the kind of wife, mother, daughter, friend, and co-worker that would honor Your name. Help me to change the world around me by becoming the woman that you long for me to be. In Jesus Name, Amen.

Be A Part of Your Love Story . . .
Long Before Your Prince Ever Comes

One of greatest gifts that the Lord gave to me during my single years was that He taught me to think, pray, and act on behalf of my future husband long before I would even know his name. You may wonder how it could be possible to be a part of your love story long before your Prince ever comes. I can assure you that it is possible and quite thrilling at that.

The first step is to realize the type of man you'd like or better yet the type of man that God would have you marry. I came to the conclusion that I didn't really know what kind of man I was looking for or how to recognize him even if he did show up. I decided to draft a list detailing the ideal qualities of a future husband. Additionally, I wanted to make sure that this list was biblically sound and in line with the kind of guy that God had in mind for me.

My Future Husband

Think about the type of man that you would like to marry one day. What qualities would you like for him to have? Pray and ask the Lord to show you what is important to expect from a young man who wants to pursue you. I encourage you to spend this time focused on inward qualities because those are the ones that last long after a person's physique fades. It is a given that you want to be attracted to this man, but for now, let's be more concerned with what his heart looks like. Don't forget to look for these qualities in the young man with whom you choose to spend your time.

1.
2.
3.
4.
5.
6.
7.
8.
9.
10.

11.
12.
13.
14.
15.
16.
17.
18.
19.
20.

Feel free to add to this list as you think of additional important qualities. Once you have a standard established, refuse to settle for less than this man of godly character.

Love Letters to My Husband

A fun and satisfying idea that I learned from precious mentors was the notion of writing love letters to my future husband while I was waiting for him to come along. I thought it was a great way to turn my mind toward my own love story. On lonely nights when it seemed everyone else had somewhere to be and someone to date, I would write letters. I was surprised how fulfilling it was to invest my time into these declarations of affection. At first I would write letters and cards and keep the envelopes in a box and then I bought a journal in which I mounted the envelopes so they could be easily opened. I would also clip and paste articles and pictures depending on what I was thinking about or involved in for that particular day. On a few of the pages, my letters were like journal entries. Brian graciously permitted me to share portions of these personal letters from me with you.

February 14, 2009

I wonder what you are doing today and if you have thought about us. Do you dream about us like I do? I wish for you the very best of days today. Once again, I release you into the Lord's hands. I know that He is keeping watch over you. I wanted you to know that I am thinking of you. You are my 'Knight in Shining Armor.' I look forward to the day when you will ride into my life and nothing will ever be the same again. Are you already in my life and I don't know it or are you yet to come? Either way, I wait for you, Prince. Come find me.

-Love, Amber

October 23, 2010

Brian,

I have been writing letters to my future husband (you) for years now. I want you to know that I have loved you long before I ever knew your name. You have become dear to me and I am excited that you are the one I wholeheartedly believe God has chosen to be my husband. I hope that I may please you and that our marriage will bring you great joy. I have saved myself for you, Brian. I love you!

-Love, Amber

Prayers for My Husband

February 13, 2002

Tomorrow is Valentine's Day. It's the first one that has come in which my thoughts and my heart are set on you. I wonder where you are. I wanted to tell you that already my heart is yours. I know when the Lord does bring us together; it will be 'joy unspeakable.' Until then, we are connected by Him. I pray for you and it's in those times that I feel close to you.

–Love, Amber

It was often that many of those journal entries throughout the years turned from letters into prayers. Ladies, one of the most powerful ways to be a part of your love story now is to pray for your future husband. This can help you to feel connected to him and the future life that you will have together. When you invest your time in prayer for your husband, you become invested in him. I believe that this leaves you less susceptible to giving your heart away frivolously. It will have to be an act of God for a man to capture your heart because your heart is already engaged and focused on the one God is going to bring to you.

When Brian and I got together and eventually married, we talked a lot about our lives and experiences, our good times as well as our most difficult times. One such time in his life which was particularly difficult came when a long-sought-after dream of Brian's was on the verge of fruition. It was at the tip of his fingertips when in an unforeseen turn, the opportunity that had previously looked promising was gone. This left him feeling pretty disillusioned and broken. The death of this dream was wrenching. In looking back over my journals, I found that during that same time period I had been praying for my husband. Here are a few excerpts from those timely entries:

10/9/08

Lord, I feel impassioned to pray for my husband right now. I pray that you would open up steel doors that have been barred in front of him, so that he can minister before You. Preserve him.

10/12/08

I pray protection today over my husband's mind. Let him be totally surrendered to You and let his ears be attentive to Your voice.

10/18/08

Lord, please protect my husband today. Bless the work of his hands. Bless his finances. Please put a guard over his mind and heart. Let him not be seduced by anyone or anything. Get us ready for the great coming together that You are planning.

Even though I was not physically connected to this difficult time in Brian's life, I was connected in the spirit realm. I found it quite a beautiful gift that I was able to share in his life. We were tied together by the unseen hand of the same God we were both actively serving.

Then days before he came into my life for good, this was a prayer written in my journal about Brian:

12/19/09

Lord, please secure my husband. Fill him with a renewed mind and heart. Let him walk in great victory today. I pray for a great turnaround in his life. Pull him up close to You. May he look, talk, and love like You. Open up the doors that he has been praying for.

We didn't realize that less than a month later, the Lord would use His mighty hands to open the doors that Brian had long been praying for—the doors that led to a family of his own. Do you see how powerful your prayers are as a future wife? Without knowing how to pray, the Holy Spirit will allow you a glimpse into your husband's heart as He guides you to pray about events or intimate hopes and dreams that most people presently in your future husband's life may not even know about.

A Prayer List

How about making a list of things you'd like to pray about for your future husband? Write those ideas in the extra spaces provided below and refer to this during your prayer time each day.

Lord, I pray that you would bless and protect my husband in his:

1. Spiritual Walk   6.
2. Purity   7.
3. Dreams and Direction   8.
4. Godly Character   9.
5. Finances   10.

Certainly your husband would benefit by intercession from the woman who will be most intimately connected to him more than any other. Never underestimate the power of a praying *future* wife.

Dream a Little Dream

If you are like me, then you have been dreaming about your wedding day since you were a little girl. Perhaps you too acted out this scenario using your childhood dolls or maybe you have daydreamed about what you hoped this special day would look like. In "The Princess Within" camps, one of my favorite activities is creating "The Wedding Collage." This is a collage of pictures clipped from various bridal magazines. The young ladies will pick out a wedding dress as well as shoes, a wedding cake, bridesmaid dresses, and colors that she dreams of using in her future wedding. I think it helps to be able to dream a little and to have an actual picture of your goal in front of you. On the days when the wait seems harder than others, this visual reminder can inspire you again and you can know that you are not on hold, but actively waiting and watching for God to do amazing things in your life. In order to help get you started, how about answering the following questions?

What colors would you like to use in your wedding?

Where would you like to have your wedding? In a church? Outdoors?

What time of year would you like to be married?

Who would you choose as your bridesmaids?

Anything extra special you'd like to do in your ceremony or use as decoration?

Your dreams are safe in the hands of your loving Father, God, who adores his little girl and delights to bless and give only the best of gifts (Luke 11:11-13). Do not be afraid to place those dreams in His hands. He has a plan and through the good days and the not as favorable, I believe that He will reveal how close He was and how faithful He remained throughout your whole story. I believe this because I have seen it proved true.

While I wholeheartedly encourage you to be a part of your love story long your prince ever comes, of course I must caution you at the same time to proceed at a balanced pace. Keep in mind that we never want to get so consumed with what is ahead that we forget to get busy serving and living fully for God right now. One day, as in the story of Ruth, God will cause your Boaz to come at just the right time. Oh, I can hear him say, "Who is that young woman over there?

AMBER GALLAGHER

I have heard everything . . . may the Lord, the God of Israel, under whose wings you have come to take refuge, reward you fully for what you have done" (Ruth 2:5,11-12). Oh, dear sister, I am excited for what, or perhaps for this chapter, I should say *who* is to come!

Purity and Relationships

12

Abstinence Makes the Heart Grow Fonder

She saw me standing in line at the restaurant my family likes to frequent about every Friday night. I knew this young girl recognized me from recently speaking in her health class the moment she exclaimed, "Mom! That's the 'Sex Lady!'"

"What?" came her mother's confused reply.

"Yeah! *This* lady came into our class and told us ALL about sex!"

I could see her mother was trying to process it all when she turned to me with quite a bit of . . . intensity. "WHAT?!"

"No, no. I'm not the 'Sex Lady.' I am the 'Abstinence Lady.' You know—save sex until marriage and follow your dreams and goals. We encourage 'No sex!'" I tried to reason a little frantically.

"Ohhh, okay." She softened her tone. "Well then, what a great message. You should be in all the schools. Teens really need a message like that . . ."

As she continued to speak, I sighed internally, "Whew, that was a close call."

"Abstinence Lady" is a name that the students in our area coined after seeing me come in and out of their classrooms, year after year, presenting a message about making positive life choices. The main theme of these presentations, you may have guessed, is to discuss the importance of practicing abstinence. Be it at the mall, the grocery store or sitting down to dinner at a restaurant, I don't think a week goes by without me hearing that all-too-familiar inquiry, "Hey, aren't you the Abstinence Lady?"

One of the Greatest Commitments

Abstinence is one of the greatest commitments you can make to maintain healthy relationships as well as to build your own character. Saving sexual activity until marriage (abstinence) is a good way to train yourself in faithfulness long before you ever meet your husband. It means that you are committed to practice self-control and say no to sex at the wrong time, in the wrong place, and with the wrong person (i.e., not your husband).

Keep in mind that there will be times in marriage when this same self-control will be necessary. For instance, you will abstain if either of you have to be absent from the home in cases of business travel or perhaps abstaining is necessary in times of sickness or other physical complications like contracting a severe case of poison ivy that spreads itself over your whole body and in turn swells and hurts and lasts for over a month. (Yes, I am deathly allergic!) In order to remain faithful in these times, you must have developed the habit of self-control and the discipline of waiting until you can come together again. This self-control learned through abstinence will spill over into other areas of your life once you realize that you can put your mind to something and have the strength to keep that commitment. It will foster respect and a life marked by peace. Surely, it's a better life when you can lay your head on the pillow at night without having uneasy feelings of regret, guilt or dread because of some out-of-control choice made that day.

Additionally, this commitment to abstinence protects you from a slew of unnecessary consequences. Many people I have met who have become sexually active are hiding that fact from their parents and those they care about. They often become deceptive about where they spend their time. These individuals seem to constantly worry about getting found out, spinning their wheels trying to figure out how to get from one lie to another, all the while feeling guilty and anxious about possible consequences lurking around the corner. This brings great tension into the home as a lady sets herself up against parents, mentors, and their standards. Several friends of mine who are mothers of teenagers have described to me times when they have felt the Lord give them warnings and direction about a wayward son or daughter, exposing plans that were going on behind their backs.

Other possible consequences include contracting sexually transmitted infections or becoming pregnant. Some of these infections can wipe out a person's ability to have children in the future or cause lifelong damage with incurable or deadly symptoms. Meanwhile, pregnancy outside of a marriage relationship can often lead to having to give up on dreams or living in poverty. I've had friends who had to drop out of school and were never able to go back and finish their career dreams, which has affected their ability to provide for themselves and their children. I have heard testimonials of young ladies who were desperate to obtain formula so that their babies wouldn't starve; mothers have wrapped their babies in t-shirts for lack of diapers or used laundry baskets and dresser drawers as cribs due to their poverty-stricken condition. It doesn't have to be this way.

Practicing abstinence can certainly protect your reputation too. When a young lady shares such a powerful gift as her sexuality with a man she is not married to, she will find that it is too fragile and powerful a gift to trust with anyone except the man that God has anointed to be her husband. It seems to me that once the covenant is made between a man, a woman, and God on the wedding day, it is then that God gives them the ability and maturity to handle the valuable gift of sexuality. Any other man who promises to handle your gift carefully without the commitment of marriage is an imposter who may only mean to break your heart and toss your reputation into the den of lions. Gossip spreads dangerously quickly at the lunch table or around the water cooler.

Sexual self-control also protects you legally in areas of custody, child support, and the many problems that stem from sexual activity involving illegal age differences.

Chloe

Chloe was told by her high school boyfriend, Jason, that he would always be there for her. Once she became sexually active, he became controlling, which led to mental and physical abuse. Then, she got pregnant. Jason got scared and angry because he didn't want anyone to find out that he was having sex. He threatened to leave Chloe if she didn't have an abortion. After much agonizing over the decision, she went through with the abortion and a few weeks later he left her anyway. Chloe assumed that she and Jason were going to stay together, get married, and live happily-ever-after. In the end, she was left broken with no self-respect, no Jason, and no baby. Unfortunately, Chloe found that the life-long effects of her abortion would end up causing many years of regret, heartache, and pain.

Women, in general, have really good imaginations and intentions. It is easy to fanaticize about being married to a guy you are dating. We assume that all the lovely details will somehow come together. If we trick our brains into seeing us married to this guy, it is easier to fall to the temptation, "We're going to get married anyway, I know it! Therefore, it's ok for us to have sex." Wrong! Being a girlfriend is not the same as being a wife. Think about the unmarried people you know, perhaps those with whom you attend the same school or are involved in the same work environment. Are their lives marked by peace, joy, and spiritual contentment or do you see drama, chaos, and separation from God? When I ask this question in an audience setting, I will without fail see multitudes of listeners adamantly shaking their heads as if to say, "Yes, we've seen the drama."

God has such amazing plans for you and for this gift of sex that HE created. This was not a gift meant to cause such chaos, pain, and brokenness. It was given to us for our good and for His glory. Sex does just that when it is used the way God designed it to be used, which is safely within the boundary of marriage. The Lord has actually given much direction in His Word about His purposes for sex: Be fruitful, multiply, and join together (bond).

Be Fruitful and Multiply

As for you, be fruitful and increase in number; multiply on the earth and increase upon it. (Genesis 9:7 NIV)

Sex is the beautiful and enjoyable way in which God has chosen to bring babies into this world. He allows mother and father to participate with Him in the creation of another little human being. What a gift!

The current trend is to perceive children as a nuisance, an inconvenience, and even a disease in need of a cure. Women are encouraged to get rid of babies if they deem that having children doesn't fit their personal comfort or agenda.

It is not hard to notice how God feels about children—they are a source of joy and happiness (Psalm 113:9). He calls them a gift and declares that a man who has many children is truly blessed (Psalm 127, Matthew 19:13-15, Malachi 2:15). The Bible goes on to further tell us that God is the Creator of all mankind, "fearfully and wonderfully" knitting us together in our mother's womb (Genesis 1, 2:7, Psalm 139). In Psalm 139:14, the word "fear" comes from the Hebrew word, *yare'*, which means "to stand in awe of, reverence, honor or respect."[1] Can you imagine that? When God formed you, He did so in awe, with honor and the utmost respect for what was taking place. Yes, children are a sacred creation of God's.

Bond to One Another

God clearly defines that another biological purpose for sex is to bring a husband and wife together in a powerful and permanent bonding experience.

Therefore a man shall leave his father and mother and be joined to his wife, and they shall become one flesh. (Genesis 2:24 NKJV)

Drink water from your own cistern, And running water from your own well. ¹⁶*Should your fountains be dispersed abroad, Streams of water in the streets?* ¹⁷*Let them be only your own, And not for strangers with you.* ¹⁸*Let your fountain be blessed, And* **rejoice with the wife** *of your youth.* ¹⁹*As a loving deer and a graceful doe, Let her breasts satisfy you at all times; And always be enraptured with her love.* (Proverbs 5:15-19 NKJV, emphasis added)

This passage in Proverbs gives instruction for a man to keep his sexuality for his own wife. A man is blessed when he sexually rejoices in his wife and not in another woman. Her breasts alone are to satisfy him and he is to be enraptured by her love and her body.

Scientists have discovered that when engaging in sexual activity, the body releases certain hormones which create a permanent emotional attachment or bond between two people.

Joe McIlhaney and Freda McKissic Bush describe this bonding in their book *Hooked: New Science on How Casual Sex is Affecting Our Children*:

When two people touch each other in a warm, meaningful, and intimate way, oxytocin is released into the woman's brain. The oxytocin then does two things: Increases a woman's desire for more touch and causes bonding of the woman to the man she has been spending time in physical contact with. This desire for more touch and the bonding that develops between a man and a woman often leads to the most intimate of physical contact, sexual intercourse. With sexual intercourse and orgasm, the woman's brain is flooded with oxytocin, causing her to desire this same kind of contact again and again with this man she has bonded to. [This] often results in long-term connectedness... Bonding is real and almost like the adhesive effect of glue—a powerful connection that cannot be undone without great emotional pain.[2]

The authors further describe an additional bonding hormone in a man called, vasopressin.

Vasopressin seems to have two primary functions related to relationships— bonding of the man to his mate and attachment to his offspring.[3]

God made our bodies to bond permanently to our husbands and vice versa. Going outside of marriage has a heartbreaking effect on our emotions as the *inability to bond after multiple liaisons is almost like tape that loses its stickiness after being applied and removed multiple times.*[4] This intense bonding ability should be preserved and protected.

The Myths of Sex Outside of Marriage

This world certainly bombards you with messages that encourage you to give yourself away before marriage. They tout myths like:

Everybody's doing it.

That's not true! In reality, a study of high schools students found that more than half had reported they are remaining abstinent.[5] A majority of students are not having sex. In fact, there are students and adults alike who are making a stand for Christ in this area of sexual purity. I encountered a young lady who was in college and a youth leader at a church where I happened to be speaking. She approached me after my talk and introduced her boyfriend. This woman let me know that she had seen me speak about abstinence several years ago when she was in seventh grade and all these years later, she and her boyfriend were committed and were successfully keeping themselves until marriage. A few months ago, I met a another woman in her twenties while shopping at the mall. She looked at me and with a tilt to her head asked, "Did I see you speak at my high school?" She shared how the abstinence message had positively affected her decisions and she was committed to living in purity. The truth is "everybody" is not having sex!

Nothing will happen to me.

That's not true! A person will ALWAYS be affected by sex in one way or another. National data shows that more than 750,000 teen girls in the United States become pregnant each year and approximately 8,000 teenagers contract sexually transmitted infections every day.[6,7] I also recently had a meeting with a young nursing student who happens to intern in the clinic of a nearby university. She expressed her deep concern at the overwhelming amount of students coming into their facility who had contracted sexually transmitted infections. The consequences are real. We cannot make poor choices and expect that we are exempt from the negative outcomes. That is not the natural order of things.

We love each other and this is how to show it.

That's not true! Love means you are willing to put yourself aside in order to do what is best for another person. Think about it. If some guy is trying to persuade you to have sex, is he really protecting or doing what is best for you? Do you think that anyone who would put you at risk for out-of-wedlock pregnancy, sexually transmitted infections or deep emotional heartache is someone who *loves* you? No way! Be brave enough to walk away and hold out for real love.

It's better to live with a person before you get married, so that you can get to know them.

That's not true! You can discern a person's character by the way they practice integrity as well as how they treat others. This can be observed in the context of friendship. The Bible says that we can know if a person is a genuine follower of Christ by intentionally noticing the fruit of their godly lives, decisions, and actions (Matthew 7:15-20). The question to ask is: "Does this individual passionately and unwaveringly follow Christ?"

Also, keep in mind that research shows couples who live together before marriage report less satisfaction in their relationships, more domestic violence, and a greater risk of divorce than couples who live separately before saying their vows.[8]

Renewed Abstinence

I had just finished an abstinence talk at one of our local schools. On my way out, I decided to take the elevator instead of trying to lug my huge cart of supplies up the stairs. As I stepped in ready to call it a pretty successful day, the doors began to close. That's when something strange happened. The doors wouldn't close all the way. I tried pressing the buttons. The door would open about five inches only to close again. Uh oh. Being stuck on an elevator was one of the things I had dreaded in life and until this moment had successfully been able to avoid. I called for help on the elevator phone and the lady on the other end assured that she would send someone for me. She seemed pretty calm about it, which helped me to feel a little less frightened. However, as time dragged on, my confidence began to waver as students began to walk by asking, "Are you stuck in there?"

"Um, yes. Would you let the office know that I'm still stuck? I'm pretty sure someone should have been here by now." I answered, trying not to sound frantic.

One poor girl couldn't stop laughing each time the door would open and close, though she assured me that she felt quite terrible about my predicament. I couldn't help but chuckle at her outbursts. Okay, it was a *little* humorous.

Needless to say, I am at home typing on my computer, so you know I eventually made it out of that elevator. Fortunately, I wasn't stuck in there too long before help did arrive and I was able to move on with my day. I have, however, made up my mind that next time I'll take a different course and use the stairs.

The fact is that we have all gotten ourselves into circumstances that have left us feeling convicted, guilty, and at times stuck, especially when it is a scenario were we have chosen to leave God's path to follow our own course. We'll ask ourselves in exasperation, "What have I gotten myself into?" We might feel uncertain as to how we will ever get out and change our ways. I have good news. You can make a fresh commitment to guard your sexuality and live God's way right now. I call this "renewed abstinence." You may have also heard it called "renewed virginity" or "secondary virginity." All of those titles are to encourage the same outcome—to begin again. The Bible says that if we "confess our sins," God is "faithful and just and will forgive us our sins and purify us from all unrighteousness." (See 1 John 1:9 NIV.) Now, that *is* good news. He makes all things new. You, dear sister, are not stuck after all. It's time to step off of the elevator headed to a disastrous nowhere; take a different course, and get on with living out God's purpose for your life.

Perhaps you'd like to take a moment to offer a prayer of repentance, confessing anything that has separated you from God and His plans for you. For some, these "sin memories" may have been bugging you since you started this chapter. Why not confess them to God this instant and let them go for good? He is faithful to forgive and offer a fresh start.

God, I am sorry for the things I have done that have broken Your heart. (Go ahead and name whatever you can remember.) Just as Your Word encourages us to do, I ask You now to forgive me. I confess that You are Lord and I ask You to cleanse me from the guilt of sin. Please replace my guilt and separation from You with peace and a restored relationship with You. Save me, even from myself, and help me to get on the right path—Your path for me. Please teach me how to choose Your way. Help me to stand strong and not to go back to my old habits. In Jesus' Name, I ask these things and I thank You for this forgiveness and new-found freedom in You. Amen.

Boundaries for the Abstinent Life

You may find the following boundaries to be helpful as they offer a practical guide to successfully living out the abstinent lifestyle.

1. Make up Your Mind

Simply let your 'Yes' be 'Yes,' and your 'No,' 'No.' (Matthew 5:37a NIV 1984)

The first step is to make a decision to live for Christ and choose to save sexual activity until marriage. I'd be remiss if I didn't give you a friendly word of warning: if you do not make this decision for yourself, someone will inevitably try and decide this for you. You may want to sign a commitment card or write this decision to practice abstinence in your journal or someplace where you will see it and be constantly reminded to "stay the course."

2. Let People Know

Instead speak the truth in love, growing in every way more and more like Christ, who is the head of his body, the Church. (Ephesians 4:15 NLT)

Once you have made up your mind to practice abstinence, it is essential to let the people around you know about your decision, whether that be your friends, family or a romantic interest. Once this reputation of Christ-centered purity is out there, it will do much to ward off anyone who is not interested in practicing abstinence. It makes living this standard much easier when people know that you will not bend to their pressure. If in conversation with a young man, you find that he is not into abstinence or shies away from being your friend after learning your standards, then that should be a huge glaring stop light. It is better to find this out early on.

I was a senior in high school when I met a handsome guy who was interested in me. Unfortunately, I felt flattered despite his reputation not lining up with God's standard. I knew that he was certainly NOT the type of guy I dreamed of marrying one day, but in my naivety I thought it would be enough to let him know early on that I was a Christian and had chosen abstinence. However, after making my standard known, he abruptly began to distance himself from me.

Several years later, when I was a college student, the same guy came into the restaurant where I was working. In less than five minutes of small talk, it was obvious that he still wanted nothing to do with God. He was quite proud to share that he was living with a girl to whom he was not married and she was pregnant. I politely listened and when we finished our conversation, I felt such a remarkable sense of gratefulness and sheer relief that this guy had distanced himself from me all those years back.

3. Say "No" to Drugs and Alcohol

Be sober, be vigilant; because your adversary the devil, as a roaring lion, walketh about, seeking whom he may devour. (1 Peter 5:8 KJV)

In addition to your decision to practice abstinence, I would encourage you to commit to completely refrain from drugs and alcohol. When people are under the influence, they obviously do not think clearly and are more prone to make poor choices. Studies have shown that high numbers of people have first-time sexual encounters, contract sexually transmitted infections, and become pregnant while under the influence of alcohol.[9] It's time to get serious about staying under God's control when it comes to behavior and decision making. When drugs or alcohol are in control, we are left to our human tendencies and the suggestions of the devil and that is never a good scenario.

4. Set a Physical Limit

But put on the Lord Jesus Christ, and make no provision for the flesh, to fulfill its lusts. (Romans 13:14 NKJV)

It is important to have a physical limit set in your mind. If a sexual encounter occurs, there are always behaviors that have led or progressed to that encounter. Sex never "just happens" contrary to the old cliché. The following chart shows the typical steps that lead to a sexual encounter:

The Steps to Physical Intimacy

Conversation
Hug
Holding Hands
Simple Goodnight Kiss

(The Heat is Turned Up!)
Passionately Kissing
Roaming Hands
Hands Under Clothing
Sex (of any kind)

It is vital to note that at the point of a passionate kiss, the heat gets turned up. Keep in mind that your body has an instinct to want to reproduce. When you are married, you want the senses to be aroused so that you can engage in sexual activity that will lead to bonding and baby making. When you are not married, you cannot afford for your body to take you down this track. It is hard to get a speeding freight train to slam on the breaks and it is extremely difficult to stop your body from charging into sexual behaviors when you allow your engine to get revved up.

In addition, it is vital to remember that any kind of physical touch will eventually leave you longing for the next step. This is dangerous in our quest to remain physically pure. Brian and I understood that as the physical element was introduced into our friendship, things could become intense. We made the decision to save kissing on the lips for our wedding day when the pastor would pronounce that we were man and wife. It was not easy to be sure, but it was absolutely worth it.

Marriage should be honored by all, and the marriage bed kept pure, for God will judge the adulterer and all the sexually immoral. (Hebrews 13:4 NIV)

If dating or courtship is about finding a mate and physical intimacy was made by God for that mate inside of MARRIAGE, then why would we mistakenly assume that physical intimacy without a covenant in place would actually help grow a relationship? Not only is risk heightened when the physical is introduced, but so is complication and drama which works to destroy any semblance of peace and purity in perhaps a previously flourishing relationship. The question we really have to be honest about answering is "Do we want God's plan for us or don't we?" It's time for you to make a decision. In the previous "Steps to Physical Intimacy" chart, please take a moment and place a star next to the step in which you are determined to stop.

5. Say "No" to Tempting Locations and Situations

I have refrained my feet from every evil way, that I might keep thy word. (Psalm 119:101 KJV)

Thy word is a lamp unto my feet and a light unto my path. (Psalm 119:105 KJV)

Abstain from all appearance of evil. (1 Thessalonians 5:22 KJV)

Learn to discern whether a situation has the potential of turning into something tempting and refuse to go there. Obvious places to stay away from include, but are not limited to: parties where people could be involved with alcohol, drugs, and sex or being anywhere alone with each other (e.g., parked cars, couches, back row at the movie theatre). It is important to keep your relationships out in the public (e.g., malls, restaurants, museums, putt-putt, theatre, ball games, group outings, family nights). Please, do not be careless or lenient in this area simply because you have done really well for a while. That is never justification to put down your guard or lower a standard.

6. Dress Classy Not Trashy

I also want women to dress modestly, with decency and propriety. (1 Timothy 2:9a NIV)

The way that we dress sends a message to other people about us. For instance, I can often tell what sport people play, places they have visited or bands they listen to by simply observing their clothing. People will make all kinds of assumptions about us based upon what they see us wear. Therefore, when a lady wears immodest clothing—short shorts/skirts, low-cut tops, midriff-revealing shirts, what message is she sending and what assumptions are people making about her?

My niece, Lexy, is such a sweet little girl who has a real longing, as we all do, to be noticed. She will sometimes break into a really loud song or even call your name out several times if your attention is directed elsewhere. Once she has your full attention, she will oftentimes want nothing more than to say "Hello."

Oh yes, whether five or ninety-five, we long to be noticed, don't we? John and Stasi Eldredge, in their book *Captivating*, identify this longing as a result of being created in the image of God. They capture the heart of the matter perfectly in their insightful determination that, just like God, "every woman longs to be swept up into a romance, to play an irreplaceable role in a great adventure, and to have a beauty to unveil—to be the Beauty of the story."[10]

In the desperation to be noticed and to unveil a unique beauty, a lady will wear an outfit that shows cleavage, belly, and backside. Sadly, she operates under the assumption that anything drawing attention generates value. Yes, we all have a keen desire to be cared about, noticed, and valued by others, but his does not come by dressing immodestly. Our value comes from God, who made us and is enamored with us. Dear sister, it is important to remember that whatever "bait" you use to try and catch a "fish" will always determine what type of "fish" comes chasing after you. Believe me, the guy who is allured by your body parts is not going to be a guy who is interested in respecting and protecting you. The scenario with a guy like that will play out quite differently. I have a little phrase I say to the girls I teach, "Dress classy, not trashy." God notices you and when the time is right, He will cause your future husband to notice the beauty that God has known you to be all along.

7. Think and Speak with Integrity

Finally, brothers and sisters, whatever is true, whatever is noble, whatever is right, whatever is pure, whatever is lovely, whatever is admirable—if anything is excellent or praiseworthy—think about such things. (Philippians 4:8 NIV)

It is vital in this world where a person is constantly bombarded with impure suggestions and godless messages, to constantly renew the mind by spending time with the Lord and by actively pursuing a pure and God-honoring thought life. Whatever you dwell on will eventually determine your actions. We are called to fill our minds with the Truth of God's Word which is always pure, lovely, admirable, excellent, and praiseworthy.

Don't use foul or abusive language. Let everything you say be good and helpful, so that your words will be an encouragement to those who hear them. (Ephesians 4:29 NLT)

Based upon this passage, all of our words should be good, helpful, and encouraging to others. Anything outside of this standard is considered foul and abusive. Additionally, the Bible tells us in Proverbs 18:21 (NLT) that "the tongue can bring death or life and those who love to talk will reap the consequences." If you consider it, the way we talk is powerful. What we say to and about others can literally either kill a person's self-esteem or encourage them and infuse hope. We have got to watch our words at all times!

8. Seek Accountability

Whoever disregards discipline comes to poverty and shame, but whoever heeds correction is honored. (Proverbs 13:18 NIV)

Stern discipline awaits anyone who leaves the path; the one who hates correction will die. (Proverbs 15:10 NIV)

Godly influences are a vital part of walking out purity in our lives. Check in with a trusted spiritual leader. Give this person permission to ask blunt questions about you and your boundary keeping as well as about the health of your relationship with God. Do not take offense if they point things out to you that are questionable. Weigh their words next to scripture and do not despise their suggestions.

Plans fail for lack of counsel, but with many advisers they succeed. (Proverbs 15:22 NIV 1984)

"The Best Sex Ever!"

One of my favorite parts of the "abstinence talk" is when I get to discuss the benefits of marriage and more specifically that studies have shown married people are the ones who report having "more sex and a better quality sexual relationship than do single, divorced or cohabiting individuals."[11] Now that is something worth looking forward to. I will usually close this part of my presentation by simply stating, "Miss Amber is actually telling you how to have the best sex ever!"

Once, in a classroom, while I was sharing this exciting bit of information, a student raised his hand. He was a young man who was vocal about his disinterest in choosing an abstinent lifestyle. I could almost tell what was about to ensue when I said, "Yes?"

"Yeah, Miss Amber, you are saying that married people have the best sex. I don't think so. I don't believe that."

"Okay, well it's backed up by research but I can't make you believe it." I thought to myself, "I wonder where you've done your research?"

I unexpectedly received an answer for my inner musings. "My uncle says once you get married, nobody has sex. Why would I want to get married?" He sat back defiantly and crossed his arms in front of his chest.

"Your uncle? Well, do you mind if I ask you a few questions about him?" I inquired as a plan was coming together in my mind. It was as if the Lord were handing to me on a silver platter the truth that would make itself clear to this confused and misled young man.

"Sure," he replied.

"Okay, then tell me . . . how does your uncle treat his wife? Does he treat her with kindness, respect, honesty, and loyalty? Does he communicate with her in a way that causes her to feel loved, important, and cherished?"

You might already know how he answered my inquiry: "No, he doesn't."

"Well, then how *does* he treat his wife?" I asked in earnest.

"He's mean and cruel. He walks all over her," he explained.

"Hmm . . . then I can understand why your uncle never has sex. You cannot treat a woman with cruelty and expect that she would want to be anywhere near you. Instead, if a husband treats his wife well and takes care of her emotionally, then a wife in that position will want to be as close to her husband as she possibly can be, if you know what I mean?"

For the first time in his life, the truth finally struck him hard. As his face registered his understanding, he replied, "You know, Miss Amber, I've never thought about it like that."

The rest of our presentation went smoothly. Instead of this young man trying to debate the truth at every turn, he became energetic and excited about being involved in the discussion and activities. I will never forget that day. Abstinence and self-control finally made sense to this young guy and you could see the freedom of that truth written all over his new countenance. What a turnaround.

Where are you at today, might I ask? Do you realize that it is essential for you to make a firm decision and establish good boundaries which will serve to alleviate the consequences of sex outside of marriage? Do you recognize the untruths about premarital sex that remain widespread by culture and by the devil and most importantly, will you refuse to fall prey to a single one of these deceptive myths?

We often assume that we will marry and that the fairytale that we have dreamed up in our minds will come to pass. Happily-ever-afters are supernatural. They come from God alone and often do not arrive in the manner that we thought they would. Following His plans for us will always include self-control and delayed gratification, paving the way for God to write an amazing love story for our lives. In the process, we can foster a healthy respect for ourselves and for that future husband we are determined to protect by our good habits now. Abstinence truly does make the heart grow fonder.

13

Purity Is a Lifestyle

Pure means to be free from whatever *weakens* or *pollutes*.[1]

As we have previously discussed, a pure life involves much more than simply not having sex. This commitment to a pure walk must include godly decisions in every aspect of a lady's life as well as a strong determination to wake up each day and continue on this course toward purity and freedom. Remember that a pure lifestyle doesn't happen naturally, without any effort. Unfortunately, it's not even in our human nature to choose God's ways (Galatians 5:17). The good news is that our hope doesn't rest in us, but in God's sustaining love.

God's purpose for purity may surprise you. His commands to be holy are not about a list of rules to control you for His own amusement. Romans 8:28 (KJV) says that "all things work together for good to them that love God, to them who are the called according to his purpose." We must realize that anything God asks us to do or not do is always for our good and will ultimately bring Him glory. When God is honored in our lives, people can't help but be drawn to Him (John 12:32).

When you love someone, you stop asking, "Why would you expect this of me?" Instead, you begin to ask, "What else can I do to show you that I love you?"

When my husband, Brian, and I started spending time together, he would drive forty-five minutes one way to see me, even if it was only for an hour or two. We wouldn't hesitate to inconvenience our schedules in order to see or talk to one another. Once, when I lived by myself, I heard strange noises coming from outside my house at six in the morning. It was still dark and I woke up frightened. I immediately called Brian and was met with a drowsy "Hello?" Instead of getting angry that I had awakened him, he was genuinely concerned as he prayed over me. We stayed on the phone for half an hour until I was able to go back to sleep.

On a recent trip to visit my grandmother, I decided to take Brian on a historic tour of my families' former homes and hangouts. My grandma gave us a guided tour of the houses in which my grandparents and parents were born and raised, the church where my parents were married, and the old Outpost, a drive-thru hangout that provided a more-than-chance first encounter between my grandma and grandpa in 1953. We drove from my mom's hometown into the little town where my dad grew up. My grandma explained to us that my dad would walk this long trek, sometimes in the snow, to see my mom. I must say that car ride forged a deeper respect and appreciation for my dad that day.

These men didn't stop to reason that they shouldn't be made to do this; they were willing to go out of their way for the sake of love. Can we do any less when we claim to love the Lord?

The Purpose of Purity

God has personal reasons for us to live in purity. In Matthew 5:8 (NIV) the Bible says, "Blessed are the pure in heart for they will see God." He is in love with us and He wants to be seen by us. I believe that God delights to share His thoughts and plans and to reveal His love for us. We cannot be so covered in the dirt of this world that we cannot see Him (Psalm 25:14).

The Bible also says in Psalm 24:3-4 (NIV), "Who may ascend the hill of the Lord? Who may stand in his holy place? He who has clean hands and a pure heart." Not only does God want to be seen by us, but He also wants us to be free to stand in His presence. He wants to be with us.

Think about it. When you have offended a friend, doesn't it feel unsettling until things are set right again? The typical instinct is to avoid the awkwardness of being in that person's presence. Then, after the apology and extended heart of forgiveness, we can once again be at liberty in the presence of our loved one. I believe we act the same way with God. When we have missed the mark, we feel awkward and many times go to great lengths to avoid Him until we feel the separation so profoundly that we cannot bear it any longer. We cry out to God and are restored through His forgiveness. When our hearts are at peace again, we wonder why we ever waited so long to make things right.

Separation hurts God, too. He wants us to be in unbroken fellowship with Him. The pure life eliminates the wall of separation that is heartbreaking for God and too unbearable for us. We can see Christ's heartbreak over the broken relationship between Himself and the people of Jerusalem conveyed in the wrenching cry of Luke 13:34 (NLT):

O Jerusalem, Jerusalem, the city that kills the prophets and stones God's messengers! How often I have wanted to gather your children together as a hen protects her chicks beneath her wings, but you wouldn't let me.

We were made to be loved and protected in covenant relationship with Him. Anything less than that will never be satisfying.

Discovering God's Truth

I know that talking about the topic of purity will bring up all kinds of heart issues. I want to say something to any young lady reading this book who may have gone through an abusive experience, whether it has been mental, physical or sexual. Please let me tell you how much I absolutely love you and that I am sorry for every bit of pain you have endured. I know that God hurts when His little girl hurts. Jesus is near to you and will walk you through the pain if you will let Him. You are not alone!

The Lord is close to the brokenhearted; he rescues those whose spirits are crushed. (Psalm 34:18 NLT)

Oftentimes, when we experience trauma in our lives, it is assured that we will pick up negative thoughts and even lies that we now believe about ourselves or our situations (e.g., "It was my fault; I will hurt for the rest of my life; I cannot trust anyone.").

Please take time to pray right now. Ask God to search your heart and see if there are any painful lies or false claims you need to release to Jesus. Please write anything that comes to your mind in the chart below under the "LIES" heading. Then, take a moment for each lie and ask God to reveal His truth to you. As you feel God speaking to your heart, write down what God is saying to you under the heading, "GOD'S TRUTH." God's truth is important for your heart and mind because the Bible says in John 8:32 (NIV) "Then you will know the truth and the truth will set you free."

LIES	GOD'S TRUTH
_____	_____
_____	_____
_____	_____
_____	_____
_____	_____
_____	_____

You may also want to spend time looking up Bible verses about freedom and God's promises. I recommend you write these meaningful verses on index cards and keep them close or save them in your phone set to show up as reminders throughout the day. If a thought tries to invade your mind that is not truth, pull out these scriptures and read them aloud, if that is possible. For an easy way to look up verses, you can use a helpful website like www.biblegateway.com. Also, please seek out a pastor and professional counselor with whom you can talk.

God's will is to heal you. Sometimes that healing comes in an immediate revelation and at other times He will walk you through a process. Please let Him accomplish His beautiful work in you according to His perfect plan. He knows exactly what He is doing. All of His motives are genuinely good and pure and will work for your greatest benefit as He reveals His love for you.

During the summer of 2009, I made a decision to uproot lies I had believed and pain with which I had not successfully dealt. I went through a long and glorious process of letting the Lord reveal His truth to me in my broken, dysfunctional places. I had a mental picture of my healing process. In it, I saw my heart as being like a vast field full of rocks and boulders. I couldn't plant, grow or harvest anything in this field until those rocks and boulders were dug up and discarded. I experienced such freedom as one by one the Lord removed those stony places in my heart. It was not an easy endeavor, but the relief I would experience would keep me coming back to deal with those boulders. I assure you, the joy and peace that replaces the pain is certainly worth the effort of going through this process.

For further Recommended Reading on Healing see *Healing Life's Hurts through Theophostic Prayer* by Edward M. Smith and *Lies Women Believe: And the Truth That Sets Them Free* by Nancy Leigh DeMoss.

A Spiritual Shower Every Day

You may wonder, "How in this world do we stay pure?" There is much temptation and overwhelming immorality all around us. The

Bible actually gives answers to this very question. It may encourage you to know that many of our Biblical heroes lived right in the middle of some pretty wicked cultures. Remember the whole Sodom and Gomorrah episode? (See Genesis 18-19.)

Keep reading. There is good news! In this world, there is a way to make a stand for God and to live the pure life. It happens through our relationship with Christ. Through His death on the cross, Jesus has become our "righteousness, holiness, and redemption" (1 Corinthians 1:30). The Bible even tells us that because of Jesus, we can "become the righteousness of God" (2 Corinthians 5:21).

How can we become this righteousness? First by accepting what Jesus did on the cross for us and further, we take on Christ's attributes of holiness and righteousness by spending time with Him.

As we have discussed in previous chapters, we can spend time with Christ through conversation (prayer) and by reading His love letters to us (Bible).

How can a young person stay pure? By obeying your word. (Psalm 119:9 NLT)

The Bible says that we can be "washed with water through the word" (Ephesians 5:25-27). How much do you physically shower to wash the dirt of the world off you? For me it's at least daily. I may have gone a day without showering before, but quite honestly I can't stand it. Even going a day, I start to feel what I call "stale." In those times, I cannot wait until I can be cleansed again.

God lets us know that in the same way that we need physical showers, more importantly and spiritually speaking, we need a shower every day in His Word. Getting into God's presence washes, renews, and refreshes us so that we can get on in our day without being distracted by a world that threatens to gradually cover over our "spirit woman" with the grimy film of compromise, temptation, and sin. Too many days of not getting washed makes one dirty and smelly—physically and spiritually.

King Louis XIV

The importance of purity took on a new perspective when I was on a visit to Germany. We toured a castle that was said to be the summer home of King Louis XIV. What I remember vividly about this visit was what the tour guide told us about this king as we were led through his immaculate bathroom quarters. I imagine that its grand amenities, which were intricately inlaid with gold, would have caused even Queen Victoria to swoon.

"It was known that King Louis did not like to take baths." I was brought back to our tour guide's monologue as he went on to explain, "Yes, he would only bathe maybe two times a year. In the end, a few of the King's toes rotted and fell completely off." Ugh! Even with all of this at his fingertips, he would not offer himself up to be cleansed.

I realized that the same is true of our "spirit woman." Which part of us do you think dies first without the proper and continual cleansing of our hearts and minds? We start trying to lean into sin by rationalizing, "This isn't so bad, is it?" or "What I am doing is not as bad as someone else's sin." Without our daily spiritual shower, our ears become deadened to hearing the Holy Spirit's guidance and our minds become decayed as we no longer meditate on the good and precious promises of God. Our personalities get more irritable and impatient. Eventually, our focus turns toward ourselves and away from God and others. Sadly, from there it only gets worse.

King David of the Old Testament knew the importance of a good spiritual shower in the Word, as he declared in Psalm 119:11(NIV): "I have hidden your word in my heart that I might not sin against you."

Being continuously washed in God's presence through prayer and Bible reading as well as putting His word in our hearts (memorizing scripture) are the keys to not sinning against God. In this process we are able to see God and live unashamed and peaceful in His presence.

Nothing is worth sacrificing God's peace.

-Erin Campbell, ECM Conference

14

Conquering Temptation

In his book, *A Shepherd Looks at Psalm 23*, W. Phillip Keller, a former sheep rancher, gives fascinating insight as to why followers of Christ are referred to as sheep. One such chapter really caught my attention. It was called, "You Anoint My Head with Oil." In it, he explains how important it is to anoint a sheep's head, ears, and nose with oil to protect them from parasites, including the dreaded "nose fly." He writes:

Sheep are especially troubled by the nose fly, or nasal fly as it is sometimes called. These little flies buzz about the sheep's head, attempting to deposit their eggs on the damp mucous membranes of the sheep's nose. If they are successful, the eggs will hatch in a few days to form small, slender, wormlike larvae. They work their way up the nasal passages into the sheep's head; they burrow into the flesh and there set up an intense irritation accompanied by severe inflammation.

For relief from this agonizing annoyance, sheep will deliberately beat their heads against trees, rocks, posts, or brush . . . In extreme cases of intense infestation, a sheep may even kill itself in a frenzied endeavor to gain respite from the aggravation.[1]

I found this particular excerpt interesting because in Scripture, the devil is referred to as "Beelzebub, the prince of demons" (Luke

11:5). The name "Beelzebub" actually means "the lord of demon flies or lord of the flies."[2] Isn't it unfortunately fitting that the "Lord of the Flies" likes to attack a child of God by sending a swarm of his lying nymphs to try and wreak havoc in a person's mind? His goal is to overwhelm you, pushing you to the edge of an emotional, physical or spiritual cliff. He wants you to give up, give in, and eventually self-destruct.

The enemy came at me with guns blaring. This cunning adversary knew that I would have seen him coming a mile away if he had walked up the drive to my front door, but of course that is not the way he came.

In my younger years, I would fall prey to the words that were hurled at me, be it voices of flesh and blood or the kind dealt from whispers in the wind that the Bible refers to as "spiritual forces of evil in the heavenly realms" (Ephesians 6:12). "You are stupid. You will never be loved. You have to be perfect and never mess up. You are not protected. God will hurt you. He will hold out on you" and of course his favorite threat, "I will have you!" I felt the war beat against my mind and heart as the swarm of lying flies circled, pressing on me with what felt like the force of a tornado. The Spirit of Fear overwhelmed me as I would lay my head on the pillow at night plagued with nightmares which continued for most of my childhood. I would fall asleep rebuking the enemy using my little girl sword, "In Jesus' name, Satan you have to flee." This truth was my mantra as I declared it hundreds of times while drifting to sleep with the sheet pulled over my head.

When my guard lowers even the smallest inch, I will sense that all-too-familiar rustling in the wind and that is when I have learned to call for reinforcements.

An attack came once while I was battling the flu. Yes, the devil will never fight fair. It was a continual barrage of mental assaults and horribly cruel accusations. There were those flies again. I fought. I read. I fasted. I knew the enemy was trying to penetrate my mind. It reminded me of a story in the Bible about Paul, his companions, and a demon-possessed girl. As they were trying to minister, she would walk along shouting constantly at them (Acts 16:17). That is precisely the type of assault I felt bombarding me. I would ask the Lord about it over and over. "Lord, why does this make me so weary? Why can't I simply shrug the enemy off and move on?"

One Sunday morning while the praise team was leading us in worship, the Lord gave me an answer. I closed my eyes and immediately saw a picture of the Lord and me together. We were walking through a tunnel of sorts; it oozed on every side—a never-ending sea of black tar. As we continued along, the Lord would hold out His hand and the dark tacky substance would draw back like a curtain. As I looked around this vision, I could see that none of the oozing tar was attaching itself to the Lord or to me. However, all around me, I could hear people crying out as they struggled against the tar that entangled them as a web entraps its next victim. The people would struggle against it only to give up as the blackness overtook them completely.

I believe that God allowed me to understand this vision. He was allowing the attack to be fierce so that I would know how it looked and felt to be attacked like the young men and women I talk to on almost a daily basis. Countless individuals may not recognize such a dark enemy or know how to defend themselves against his blows. Meanwhile, this adversary convinces a person that she is hopeless and that her fate is sealed by the enemy's pronouncements over her. Not so!

My first reaction when the enemy comes at me is to pray for deliverance. However, even recently, the Lord has been speaking to me about the importance of the struggle.

We can rejoice, too, when we run into problems and trials, for we know that they help us develop endurance. And endurance develops strength of character, and character strengthens our confident hope of salvation. (Romans 5:3-4 NLT)

I have learned that in this war over our souls, the enemy is a cruel and ruthless deceiver—and always has been. This war between good and evil is one that all the saints before you have waged. Everyone, especially those who have determined to live for God, has taken up arms against this ancient foe. It is a given that you and I too have the same enemy who will make a go at us. It is a surety that if we resist his every attempt and cling to Jesus, we will come out victorious every single time. God has shown us how to succeed throughout His Word. It is our survival guide. A clear promise God gives to us is that if we "resist the devil, he will flee" (James 4:7). Sister, we cannot lose with the Commander-in-Chief of Heaven's Army on our side and when your heart is overwhelmed, cry out as the Psalmist: "From the end of the earth will I cry unto thee, when my heart is overwhelmed, lead me to the rock that is higher than I" (Psalm 61:2 KJV).

What, then, shall we say in response to this? If God is for us, who can be against us? (Romans 8:31 NIV 1984)

But you belong to God, my dear children. You have already won a victory over those people, because the Spirit who lives in you is greater than the spirit who lives in the world. (1 John 4:4 NLT)

We know that we are destined to be the victors in this battle. However, in order to fight the good fight, it is important to know how the enemy will come at you. What are his tactics? He's been using the same ones for thousands of years now. Often, he does not come as the ferocious warrior with his sword drawn to slay you. Instead, he comes deceptively at times posing as "an angel of light" to tempt you, confuse you, and sway you away from God, your Source and only Protection (2 Corinthians 11:14).

Temptation Is NOT Sin

Jesus said to his disciples, 'Things that cause people to sin are bound to come.' (Luke 17:1a NIV 1984)

The first step in defeating the enemy's tactic of temptation is to recognize that temptation will come and that the temptation in and of itself is not sin. The devil even tried to tempt (lure) Jesus in a way that was contrary to God's Word. Jesus succeeded in resisting the devil and we can too.

Many have referred to our thought life as a spiritual battlefield. This is where the devil likes to try and gain the most ground in the battle over our souls. He understands that if he can sway or control the way you think, then he can control your behavior. The enemy can come up with some pretty depraved thoughts and suggestions, but do not let a single one of them take root in your mind. The devil is hoping that you will take the bait. Then, his secondary tactic comes when he tries to condemn you for these thoughts that he has hurled at you. He wants you to own them.

You are not who or what the devil says you are. God is the only One with the authority to tell you who you are. Refuse to believe any thought or claim that comes to your mind that is contrary to God's Word or His promises.

I encourage you to continue to persevere. Your foe may press you for a while, but refuse to back down. If he continues, you may get tired, but keep pressing. Include trusted prayer warriors on whom you can call to help pray through the situation or enemy assault. These beloved friends will hold your arms up when you grow weary in the fight (Exodus 17:11-12).

Previously, when the enemy would attack, I would fight until I would feel completely worn out. My husband caught onto what was going on with me and very adamantly made me promise not to fight these attacks alone, not even for a minute. We made a pact that I must call him immediately and let him pray with me. Every time my husband and I get together and pray, I feel a lifting of the attack—absolute relief. Your enemy knows that if you keep your fight a secret or try to fight alone, it will be easier for him to get the upper hand.

If you needed to call a prayer warrior who would genuinely come alongside of you in this fight, who would that be? Is there more than one person you could call? Take a moment to ask the Lord to show you a safe person that you could contact to pray with you. List those names as well as phone numbers below:

1.
2.
3.

You may also find it helpful to set a weekly phone call or visit in order to pray over needs or concerns.

Again, I tell you that if two of you on earth agree about anything you ask for, it will be done for you by my Father in heaven. (Matthew 18:19 NIV 1984)

When Temptation Comes

Sin may seem pleasurable and alluring at first, but the Bible assures us that giving in to the temptation to sin does not bring lasting joy. It may give a momentary thrill, but will assuredly produce lifelong pain and bondage.

Adam and Eve are merely two examples. That "forbidden fruit" looked really pleasing and eating it seemed like a good idea at the time, but look at what it cost them. Sin entered the world; they were expelled from a paradise of a home, and they were separated from God. No more long walks together, face to face in the cool of the day. Ouch! The fall from that tree left some pretty nasty wounds.

The temptation to follow your flesh may seem too overwhelming and it may feel as if you are the only one who has ever struggled with this. However, God has promised you that:

No temptation has overtaken you except what is common to mankind. And God is faithful; he will not let you be tempted beyond what you can bear. But

He was a murderer from the beginning, not holding to the truth, for there is no truth in him. When he lies, he speaks his native language, for he is a liar and the father of lies.

I never struggled with that lie again.

How Do We Defeat Temptation?

We understand how the enemy can mount an attack against us and that God, The Commander-in-Chief of Heaven's Army, is on our side. We also know that God has laid out a plan of defense for us in His Word. Let's recap and clearly lay out the weapons in your arsenal so that you may wield them the next time you hear a rustling swarm of flies in the distance.

First, understand that you cannot fight an enemy you do not recognize nor can you fight adequately without the proper weapons. You have heard me mention these powerful spiritual tools to you, but it never hurts to reiterate them over and again until your use of them is second nature.

Put on the full armor of God so that you can take your stand against the devil's schemes. For our struggle is not against flesh and blood, but against the rulers, against the authorities, against the powers of this dark world and against the spiritual forces of evil in the heavenly realms. Therefore put on the full armor of God, so that when the day of evil comes, you may be able to stand your ground, and after you have done everything, to stand. Stand firm then, with the belt of truth buckled around your waist, with the breastplate of righteousness in place, and with your feet fitted with the readiness that comes from the gospel of peace.

In addition to all this, take up the shield of faith, with which you can extinguish all the flaming arrows of the evil one. Take the helmet of salvation and the sword of the Spirit, which is the word of God. And pray in the Spirit on all occasions with all kinds of prayers and requests.

With this in mind, be alert and always keep on praying for all the saints.
(Ephesians 6:11-18 NIV 1984)

The weapons we fight with are not the weapons of the world. On the contrary, they have divine power to demolish strongholds. We demolish arguments and every pretension that sets itself up against the knowledge of God, and we take captive every thought to make it obedient to Christ.
(2 Corinthians 10:4-5 NIV 1984)

Secondly, it is vital to watch and pray that you may see the enemy coming. Do not be caught unaware. Time spent in God's presence will give you strength and confidence to charge and not cower in the face of an enemy attack.

Sometime back, the Denver Post reported this story: Like many sheep ranchers in the West, Lexy Lowler has tried just about everything to stop crafty coyotes from killing her sheep. She has used odor sprays, electric fences, and scare-coyotes. She has slept with her lambs during the summer and has placed battery-operated radios near them. She has corralled them at night, herded them at day. But the southern Montana rancher has lost scores of lambs—fifty last year alone.

Then she discovered the llama—the aggressive, funny-looking, afraid-of-nothing llama. 'Llamas don't appear to be afraid of anything,' she said. 'When they see something, they put their head up and walk straight toward it. That is aggressive behavior as far as the coyote is concerned, and they won't have anything to do with that . . . Coyotes are opportunists, and llamas take that opportunity away.[5]

The enemy is also an opportunist. He will watch to see if his bullying ways are going to cause you to back down or give in. Remember that when you stand firm and declare "Be gone!" to your enemy, you take away his opportunity to harass you and he must shrink back (Matthew 4:10).

Watch and pray so that you will not fall into temptation. The spirit is willing, but the flesh is weak. (Matthew 26:41 NIV)

In addition to watching and praying, fasting is an essential, powerful, and often underutilized weapon in this spiritual fray. Fasting is giving up something whether it is food, television or some other sacrifice. When we fast, it humbles and purifies us. We focus on God and ask for His movement in our lives and situations. Once, I joined my family in prayer and fasting for my nephew, Nick. My prayer was that the stronghold of the enemy would be broken and he would turn to Christ after a heartbreaking and rebellious span of several years. Four days into the fast, on a Friday at midnight, Nick said he was alone and could feel a spiritual battle raging there in his room between the Lord and the enemy. He finally surrendered his heart and life to God and was radically changed for Christ. Hallelujah!

Afterward, when Jesus was alone in the house with his disciples, they asked him, "Why couldn't we cast out that evil spirit?" (Mark 9:28 NLT)

He told them, 'This kind can come out only by prayer and fasting. (Mark 9:29 NIV)

In order to stay strong in the fight, it is important to saturate your mind in God's Word—the Bible. Again, take notice that in Matthew 4, when Jesus would overpower the enemy, His defense would always begin with "It is written . . ." You, dear sister, must have the Word in front of you and inside of you.

I use to think that I had a scripture memorization deficit. For years, I would at least yearly resolve to make a habit of memorizing the Word. I knew I needed it. I think the Lord was trying to bring to my attention that this discipline was a lifeline in my being able to take up arms against the enemy as well as essential in developing a deeper relationship with Him. Honestly, I had really good intentions; they just never amounted to much action. That is, until the enemy came at me so hard and so long that getting the Word inside of me and quoting it, many times aloud, became necessary for any ounce of mental relief. I finally took the step and began to memorize Scripture. When sensing an enemy attack, I began to respond by reciting verses I had memorized for the week. The enemy would back off EVERY time. There is no good time like the present to begin getting God's Word into your heart. You will find that it will be your comfort and your defense. Never forget that the Word is your sword (Ephesians 6:17).

This war is real. We can act as if it is not going on until we fall into the enemy's snare, or we can use wisdom and truth that God has given us to gain victory for our lives as well as for those around us. Let us declare that we will not succumb to our enemy. We will overwhelmingly conquer and by the power of God render every temptation and enemy assignment against us to be void and useless. Jesus gave us an example to show us that we do not have to fall to our enemy. It is possible, through Christ, to be victorious every time.

For we do not have a high priest who is unable to empathize with our weaknesses, but we have one who has been tempted in every way, just as we are—yet he did not sin. [16]*Let us then approach God's throne of grace to help us in our time of need.* (Hebrews 4:15-16 NIV)

One truth is absolutely certain . . .

You cannot flirt with the devil and dance with Jesus at the same time!

-Matthew Campbell, ECM Conference

15

The Mystery Behind Purity

When you walk with the Lord for any length of time, the Lover of your soul can't help but begin to reveal His heart toward you. He has always loved you, dear friend, and He wants a close and personal relationship with you. The great mystery behind God's desire for us to live in purity is not about rules, but about love. One thing I have seen many times over is that with God there is always more to the story than we can immediately see or understand.

Flee from Sexual Immorality

Flee from sexual immorality. All other sins a person commits are outside the body, but whoever sins sexually, sins against their own body. [19]*Do you not know that your bodies are temples of the Holy Spirit, who is in you, whom you have received from God? You are not your own;* [20]*you were bought at a price. Therefore honor God with your bodies.* (1 Corinthians 6:18-20 NIV)

I have always found this to be such an intriguing scripture—especially the part about how sexual immorality is the sin that is committed against a "person's own body," whereas "all other sins" are committed "outside the body." What is the difference between sexual sin and all other sin? If you think about it, sexual sin is the one offense in which our body becomes the very instrument of sin not only physically, but also spiritually, emotionally, mentally, and socially. This is an act that affects every part of who we are.

Why is it important that our bodies not become an instrument of sin? Take another look at 1 Corinthians 6:19-20 to find the answer. Did you catch it? It says that "your bodies are temples of the Holy Spirit; you are not your own" and that you were "bought at a price." Therefore, we are told to "honor God" with our bodies.

The Temple of the Most High God: A Little History

Back in the day of Moses, God victoriously freed the people of Israel from the Egyptians, to whom they were enslaved (Exodus 4-15). They left Egypt and headed for the land that God had promised would be their own. This was an amazingly lush and fertile "Promised Land." It was described as a land "flowing with milk and honey" (Leviticus 20:24) and would later become the country of Israel—home of the Israelites, God's chosen people.

It is interesting to note that if you look on a map, Egypt and Israel are pretty close to each other. This journey took them forty years when it should have only taken them days to complete (Deuteronomy 1:2). The Bible says that God did not lead them through Philistine country, which would have been a shortcut. He knew that if they had to fight their enemies for this land, they might have "changed their minds and returned to Egypt." They would have willingly returned to bondage (Exodus 13:17). It seems that God wanted the people of Israel to gain experience in walking with Him before they would be ready to inherit their promise. This journey is often referred to as the "wilderness time."

While in the wilderness, God came to Moses and told him that He wanted Moses to build a tabernacle (residence) for God so that He could dwell among the Israelites. When they would set up camp, the tabernacle would always be positioned right in the center of the people and God gave Moses instruction, to the tiniest detail, on how to build this tabernacle. Even though it would be constructed by the hands of men, the Tabernacle had to be perfectly made according to God's pattern (Exodus 25:8-9, Hebrews 8:5). That wasn't the only requirement. In addition, those who served in the tabernacle were to minister unto the Lord exactly as He commanded. This was non-negotiable.

This wilderness tabernacle was a temporary and portable dwelling to house God's presence. The Jews later built a more permanent stone temple often referred to as Solomon's Temple (1 Chronicles 22:9-10, 2 Chronicles 2:1) and then when that temple was destroyed (Jeremiah 52:12-14), they eventually built another temple commonly referred to as Zerubbabel's Temple (Ezra 6:3-4, Haggai 2:3-9). Later, a renovation caused it to be known as Herod's Temple. This was the temple standing in Jerusalem during the time Jesus walked the Earth.[1]

The pattern for these dwellings was exact in their design as each had an outer court, where everyone could come and present sacrifices to God (Leviticus 17:5); a Holy Place, where the priests would minister before God each day (Exodus 27:21); and a Most Holy Place, also known as the Holy of Holies. This was where the actual presence of God dwelt. Only the High Priest, one time per year, would go into the Holy of Holies to request atonement (covering) for his own sins as well as the sins of all the Israelite people (Hebrews 9:7).

The Holy Place and the Holy of Holies (God's presence) were separated by a huge, thick curtain or some translations even call it a veil (Exodus 40:21, Hebrews 9:3) and when Jesus died on the cross, the Bible says that this veil was "torn in two from top to bottom" (Matthew 27:50-51).

Do you understand the importance in the tearing of this veil? According to Hebrews 10:20, the veil represented Christ's body which was torn so that we could have the availability of God's presence to us. Not only one priest, one time each year, but all of us, from that moment on, had access to God. We can now approach His throne anytime with awe and reverence, but without fear or shame (Hebrews 4:16).

After Jesus' death and the veil was torn in two, the followers of Christ would become the tabernacle or temple where God's Holy Spirit would dwell. Jesus told his disciples in John 14:26 that the Father would send His Holy Spirit to dwell within them and in Acts 2, we can read that Jesus' followers were in fact filled with God's Holy Spirit. Yes, God came to live in the tabernacle of humanity to dwell in the center of us. This has been God's plan from the beginning. He has always desired to be Emmanuel—God with us!

God's Perfect Pattern

Remember that the tabernacle of God, according to the pattern of things, would have to be built, not according to men, but instead to God's perfect pattern. You may be wondering, "Then why did He choose us to house His presence? After all, we are far from perfect, right?" Take a look at what the Bible says regarding the way in which we were "built":

You made all the delicate, inner parts of my body and knit me together in my mother's womb. ^{14}Thank you for making me so wonderfully complex! Your workmanship is marvelous—how well I know it. ^{15}You watched me as I was being formed in utter seclusion, as I was woven together in the dark of the womb. ^{16}You saw me before I was born. Every day of my life was recorded in your book. Every moment was laid out before a single day had passed. How precious are your thoughts about me, O God. They cannot be numbered! (Psalm 139:13-17 NLT)

Oh, how wonderful! You, dear sister, are the creation of God! He "built" you with His own hands according to His own perfect pattern. You and I were made to be exactly who He wanted us to be.

Not only were we made with His hands according to His perfect pattern, but the Bible further lets us know that we are even created in the image of God (Genesis 1:26). The next time you look into a mirror, take a good long look and see the traces of God in your face.

May I take a moment to write to those who have possibly struggled with feeling unwanted or as if you were a "mistake"? God, Creator of all things, is the only One who has the power to breathe life in order to create a human being. (Genesis 2:7, Job 33:4) Daughter of God, take heart. Your biological mother and father may have been the vehicles that God used to bring you into this world, but you are here because God wanted you here for such a time as this and He does not make mistakes!

To the daughter who never feels "good enough": You may obsess about the way you look, your clothes or your body. Unfortunately, some of you are dying to change yourself into a version of you that isn't realistic. This constant pressure you put on yourself can often lead to feeling depressed and empty. Please pause for a moment right now to surrender this obsession to the Lord. God formed you in His image, gave you life, and He has an amazing purpose for you. You are who He created you to be. You were not created to be your best friend or your sister or the girl on the cover of the latest magazine. Your pattern had to be *perfectly* His in order for His Holy Presence to feel at home inside of you. Relax and let Him form you into the beautiful daughter that you were made to be with a captivating beauty that radiates from the inside out.

The Holy of Holies

Now that you understand your destiny is to become the temple of God's presence, let's revisit the importance of living in purity once more to add another interesting detail. I simply have to say that God is brilliant!

*It is God's will that you should be **sanctified:** that you should avoid sexual immorality;* [4]*that each of you should learn to control your own body in a* *way that is holy and honorable.* (1 Thessalonians 4:3-4 NIV, emphasis added)

In this Thessalonian verse, the word "sanctified" is the Greek word, "hagiasmos," which stems from the root word, "hagiazo" meaning to "purify, declare sacred or holy."[2,3] This is a Greek rendering of the original Hebrew word, "kodesh," which means "holiness, or set apart."[4,5,6]

Now if you remember, you have already learned that the temple of God contained three parts: The Holy Place, The Most Holy Place and THE HOLY OF HOLIES. The Holy of Holies, was the part of the temple that housed Who? _____

Did you answer that the Holy of Holies housed God's holy presence—God Himself? Good! Now get this: The Hebrew words for the Holy of Holies are "Kodesh Hakadoshim." Do you see a familiar word there? It is God's will for us to be holy, sanctified, set apart or "KODESH" because we are the "KODESH HAKADOSHIM."[7] We have become the Holy of Holies, the sacred temple of the Most High God.

Purity (holiness) is an absolute necessity for unbroken communion between us and God. We must keep these bodies pure because we are the temple of God's Holy Spirit and that must be a sacred place. This is also why Satan's goal has always been to defile the Lord's temple—so that God's presence would not dwell among the people that He loves. Why do you think the world constantly bombards an individual with exposures to sexual immorality? Our culture sexualizes everything from TV shows to movies, magazines, cartoons, and video games. Instead of falling for this seduction, we must resist the temptation to defile our bodies and instead be controlled and committed because sexual immorality defiles the Temple!

Consequently, you are no longer foreigners and strangers, but fellow citizens with God's people and also members of his household, [20] built on the foundation of the apostles and prophets, with Christ Jesus himself as the chief cornerstone. ²¹ In him the whole building is joined together and rises to become a holy temple in the Lord. ²² And in him you too are being built together to become a dwelling in which God lives by his Spirit. (Ephesians 2:19-22 NIV)

What agreement is there between the temple of God and idols? For we are the temple of the living God. As God has said: 'I will live with them and walk among them, and I will be their God, and they will be my people.' (2 Corinthians 6:16 NIV)

Never forget that you are the sacred dwelling place—the Temple of the Most High God!

How Do I Know He's "The One"?

In my lifetime, I have asked many a married woman, "How did you know that your husband was 'The One'?" Many of them responded with the typical answer, "I can't really explain it, but when it's right you just know!" Such an answer always sounded romantic yet elusive. I would think, "What if I don't know? What happens then?" It was all so mysterious.

I have come to believe that the explanation for their "knowing" stems from the fact that they had sensed God's peace in their direction and decision. Ah, now that is something I could understand because I have experienced instances when the Lord has directed and assured me of His plan. It is often in those times that I would sense a divine clarity and feel His peace settle over me serving to encourage me onward. While I had never experienced the "you just know" phenomenon, I could, however, begin to prepare and position myself to be more able to discern God's blessing of peace to give me guidance.

Many a man claims to have unfailing love, but a faithful man who can find? The righteous man leads a blameless life; blessed are his children after him. (Proverbs 20:6-7 NIV)

The measure of a man is not his looks or even how he can act temporarily, but a "worthy" man is marked by godly character and kindhearted service toward others. The Bible describes the type of man who would make a great husband in Ephesians 5:21-28 (Message):

^{21}*Out of respect for Christ, be courteously reverent to one another.*

$^{22\text{-}24}$ *Wives, understand and support your husbands in ways that show your support for Christ. The husband provides leadership to his wife the way Christ does to his church, not by domineering but by cherishing. So just as the church submits to Christ as he exercises such leadership, wives should likewise submit to their husbands.*

$^{25\text{-}28}$ *Husbands, go all out in your love for your wives, exactly as Christ did for the church—a love marked by giving, not getting. Christ's love makes the church whole. His words evoke her beauty. Everything he does and says is designed to bring the best out of her, dressing her in dazzling white silk, radiant with holiness. And that is how husbands ought to love their wives. They're really doing themselves a favor—since they're already 'one' in marriage.*

Is This Relationship Orchestrated by God?

At times, it would be clear that a certain young man was not for me based upon the qualities that I did not find in his character. For instance, the Bible clearly says in 2 Corinthians 6:14 (NIV): "Do not be yoked together with unbelievers. For what do righteousness and wickedness have in common? Or what fellowship can light have with darkness?"

If the person you are considering does not have a relationship with Jesus Christ, then he is not God's choice for you. Period. Keep in mind that even though the person you are spending time with professes to be a Christian, that does not mean he is "The One" for you. Other questions you may want to ask yourself would be "Does this relationship challenge and inspire me to grow in the Lord or do

I feel as if I am not as strong spiritually? Does he line up with the standard of godly qualities I have identified as important to me and the kind of marriage I desire to have?"

There were instances when the answer would become clear to me as I would wait, pray, and read the Bible. I would have input from trusted spiritual mentors that was invaluable to me. At other times, an answer would seem to be long in coming and I would have to submit myself and wait for God's peace and clear direction. There were friendships with "possibility" that I continued in without romantic involvement in which the Lord eventually closed the door by giving my heart or the other person's heart clarity; or God would remove the potential opportunity completely, such as the person would move away or develop feelings for someone else.

The blessing of the Lord makes a person rich, and he adds no sorrow with it. (Proverbs 10:22 NLT)

Another indication of a blessing from God is that it makes a person rich (not monetarily speaking) and He adds no sorrow with it.

I can definitely recount a couple of relationships in my journey that I wish I would've viewed in the light of this wise Proverb. There was one, in particular, that I tried hard to make happen for so many years and every attempt ended in such tearful sorrow. Shouldn't that have been a big glaring sign to me? I kept walking away because I knew that such pain, indecision, and emotional turmoil wasn't good. I would sometimes despise myself for being too "weak" to end it permanently. Now, I look back and realize I had my own brokenness that caused me to be drawn to this young man and his similar baggage. I can attest to the fact that two broken people will certainly not make a whole and healthy relationship.

I proceeded to make provision for this unhealthy relationship. I thought I could continue to run in the same circles and share in ministry with this person, but I don't believe this was a good idea because as soon as I'd find the courage to put my feelings for him away, I'd see him doing something kind and tender for someone else and think, "If only . . ." Then, once again, I would step into a frustrating cycle where "if only" was just that—a fleeting hope of something that would never come to fruition. It was only when I removed myself completely from the same social circles and interaction with this guy that I was truly able to move on and heal. It is hard to walk away from something or someone that has become a comfortable norm but when you taste freedom and healing, you will not want to live in the past one more day.

The Binder

Once my husband and I decided that we felt really good about the direction of our friendship, we wanted to concentrate on getting to know each other better to see if this was in fact leading to marriage. I introduced him to "The Binder." "What is the binder?" you may ask. Well, it is a collection of cherished devotions, interesting excerpts and quotes on relationships, as well as hundreds of questions to cover before getting engaged. I had collected these throughout the years before ever meeting my future husband. In the case of this "hopeful romantic," you might wonder if "The Binder" was a bit unromantic and rigid. I wanted to be swept off my feet, but I also wanted to be very practical and sure about this decision before my feet ever left the ground. I would say that the more you can learn early on, the better. You want to have the important information before you get your heart involved and accept a ring on your finger. Once your heart gets attached, it's hard to turn back.

When it comes to relationships, many people do a miniscule amount of background research to find out who the person they are considering really is. What is this person's relationship with the Lord truly like when they believe no one is watching or once they feel comfortable enough with you to be their true self? How does this person act with friends and family? How did they behave in their last relationship? What are their hopes and dreams? Do those coincide with your own? Oh, and if anyone questions this choice, why do we get defensive and angry? In the end, we often find out that the misgivings of parents and friends were valid after all.

This is why I believe courtship is a much better method to use in developing a relationship than dating. It helps you to have a more focused plan. A girl can slow down, take a breath, and do the necessary research during the friend stages of courtship.

When Brian and I became friends and moved through the courtship process, the more I grew to know him, the more I esteemed and admired his godly character and genuine kindness toward others and myself. As we worked our way through "The Binder," it became clear that we were on the same page with our beliefs and convictions. I came to love the man that Brian Gallagher is through our hours of conversation and interaction with each other and our respective families. If you don't know what courtship is, don't worry. We will discuss the concept of this method in the next chapter.

Meanwhile, how did I know that Brian was the one for me? Well, it's true that I had never felt so deeply before for a man in all of my life. It was also true that we had come to find that we were like-minded in so many ways, especially in our desire to love and serve God. They were right! When it happens, "you just know" it has happened because it isn't heartbreaking and burdensome, it is peaceful. The divine "knowing" comes with a nudging from the Holy Spirit, our Guide, in this particular direction. God opens the door that no man can open. In my story, it felt as if the Lord had presented my husband and me to each other. Our relationship was a gift and the Lord added no sorrow to it!

17

Courtship

Is It the Same as Dating?

That's a great question. Courtship and dating are two very different approaches to developing a romantic relationship. Dating can involve a "shopping around" mentality that may "try out" anyone who seems attractive or the least bit interesting. It often begins with a romantic intent and then friendship tends to develop over time. Several years ago, I began to question the whole dating scene. It seemed a little out of order to start giving my heart away so quickly before I knew that I could even be friends with a guy.

This dating approach may get you more Friday night dates, but it may also leave you with a broken heart. Some have also reasoned that this lifestyle could potentially set up a kind of "divorce pattern," since it practices "trying people out" and moving on whenever you are unhappy with the relationship.

You may also want to be aware that as you draw closer and closer to one another in a relationship, the physical temptation becomes more intense. Without marriage in the near future, this is a constant frustration. To be honest, I have met numerous Christians who really meant to be pure in serious relationships during high school and college. However, the more emotionally involved they got, the more physically charged the relationship became. For a woman, once the heart is united, the body begins to feel the urge to unite. This can lead to trouble. I think that's why the Shulamite girl, in love with King Solomon, was warned a few times to "not arouse or awaken love until it so desires" (Song of Solomon 2:7 NIV 1984). First she would proclaim her love and affection for King Solomon, which in turn would lead her to admit her desires to now bind herself physically with him. Ladies, since the same powerful progression is true for us, we cannot let ourselves go there before marriage. Guard your heart by not getting emotionally or physically entwined.

Dating without the intent of marriage is like going to the candy store with no money. Either you leave unsatisfied or you take something that is not yours.

-Anonymous

The courtship approach is a more protected, planned out, and focused venture. You spend your single years building a relationship with God, establishing solid friendships, working toward your dreams, and becoming the woman God longs for you to be by developing the fruit of the Spirit in your own life. Then, when you are at a point and an age where you feel ready for marriage, through God's leading, you may want to enter into a relationship. Courting begins with friendship and then romantic interest tends to develop over time as you come to know the person. In courtship, the intent and ultimate question will be: "Do I feel like you are the one God is calling me to marry?" By the time romantic and emotional bonds are being formed, you are on the steady track toward marriage. To have this goal of marriage just over the horizon really helps to steady any physical urges that threaten to be awakened.

Some of these young men with whom you have developed a relationship may simply remain as good friends. This is a natural outcome since the start of courtship begins with friendship rather than romantic interest.

A crucial element of courtship is establishing physical and emotional boundaries and inviting accountability such as parents, mentors, and other spiritual leaders to offer support through prayer and giving advice.

Take a look at the following chart that describes the levels of courtship from the beginning stages to the final stage of marriage. Notice that each level in the process of courtship contains various goals on which to focus.

The Process of Courtship

It's Jesus and Me.

Goal 1:

Foundation—The source of your life is founded upon a relationship with God. Focus on and develop your relationship with the Lord through prayer and Bible study. Learn to follow His direction.

Goal 2:

Ministry Involvement—Get involved in ministry at church or in your community. Ask God to show you His plan for your life. Begin working on your life purpose dreams.

Goal 3:

Personal Development—Cultivate a life that is marked by good character, maturity, and responsibility in your finances, work, and home. Also, participate in training opportunities, mentorships, and conferences that relate to spiritual, financial, parental or relational betterment. Become the woman of God that you long to be.

I'm kind of interested in someone.

Goal 4:

Friendship Begins—Be involved in the same group settings such as ministry teams while getting to know each other.

Goal 5:

Friendship Develops—As with any other friend, talk and share personal experiences and life purpose goals. Continue to spend time in group settings as opposed to pairing off as a couple.

Goal 6:

Friendship Deepens—Become even more acquainted in thoughts, dreams, and life goals. Only at this point will you talk to each other about whether marriage is a possibility.

I feel like he could be the one for me.

Goal 7:

Pre-Engagement—Find a pastor who will conduct pre-engagement counseling. Ask a healthy married couple, spiritual leaders, and your parents to agree to walk with you and provide counsel as well as agree to pray with you for direction and accountability in the relationship. Continue to grow closer emotionally, mentally, and spiritually.

Goal 8:

Engagement—Do you have the unreserved blessing of your spiritual mentors, parents, and pastors? Continue to develop good communication and mutual respect as you grow deeper emotional, mental, and spiritual connectedness. Seek out pre-marriage counseling.

Goal 9:

Marriage—Become one mentally, emotionally, spiritually, and now physically. Remember that the closer you grow toward God, the closer you will grow toward your spouse. Continue to learn new ways to honor and serve each other. This is a lifelong growing process. Welcome to the next chapter of your life and please enjoy the journey.

Courtship provides you with a focused plan as well as boundaries and accountability. Take your time and do the research. Remember that this is not a race to the altar. You are making decisions that you will want to be comfortable and happy about for the rest of your life. Don't forget to include family and spiritual mentors. Choosing the man you will marry is such a big decision. I personally realized that such an important choice in my life was not one I wanted to make on my own with little thought.

Plans fail for lack of counsel, but with many advisers, they succeed. (Proverbs 15:22 NIV)

Questions to Ask Before Getting Engaged

It is always a good idea to be informed. That is one way to help us make good decisions. The following is a list of questions that can serve as a guide in getting to know someone. The conversation sparked by these will help you determine if this relationship has the potential of heading toward engagement. The answers for many of these questions will be evident upon observation. Other questions will need to be asked at some point. You may also want to take some personal time to record your responses to these inquiries as he will undoubtedly want to know where you stand as well.

AMBER GALLAGHER

Spiritual Walk

How often do you go to church?

What church denomination do you prefer?

In what church denomination would you want to raise your future children?

Can I see a copy of your church's doctrine? What scripture is this doctrine based upon?

Do you live out these principles in your life?

What are your beliefs on tithing?

What does it mean to be "saved"?

Do you read the Bible every day?

Do you pray every day?

How do you feel about prayer?

Will you describe how you came to know the Lord?

Describe your current relationship with the Lord.

Are you tender to the voice as well as the things of God?

Do you think attending church is an important part of your spiritual walk?

Do you depend on God for every decision you make? By what means does God direct you?

What does being a spiritual leader of your home mean to you?

How do you feel about divorce? What do you feel are acceptable reasons for a couple to get divorced?

Would you say that your walk has had many ups and downs?

Do you feel that you could ever walk away from the Lord under any circumstance?

Do you plan to have daily devotion time with your wife and family?

Are you pro-life or pro-choice?

Do you think that it is okay for a Christian to drink, smoke, cuss, have sex or gossip?

Are you or have you ever been addicted to anything such as pornography, alcohol or drugs?

What does Ephesians 5:21-28 mean to you?

What are your thoughts about a wife "submitting" to her husband?

How many hours of music, movies, television or video games do you listen to, watch or play in an average week?

What type of music do you listen to?

Do you feel that media can influence a person's thoughts and actions?

How do you react if something inappropriate shows up in your media?

How do you protect yourself from these influences?

AMBER GALLAGHER

You

What is your educational background?

Do you strive to develop the fruit of the Spirit in your daily life?

Would you say that you are a perfectionist?

How would you react if someone put you down in front of a group of people?

How do you feel about tattoos and piercings?

How many siblings do you have? What kind of relationship do you have with them?

What was your home life like when you were growing up? How is your relationship with your parents?

Are you more attracted to physical attributes or personality?

Do you think that it is acceptable to "check out" other women while you are dating, courting or married?

What are your pet peeves?

Would you say that you have any quirky character traits?

Would you describe yourself as slightly possessive or controlling in any aspect of your life?

Would you say that your temper gets the better of you sometimes?

Have you ever thrown anything or hit anyone while upset?

Do you like to argue?

How do you feel about abstinence?

What are your physical/emotional boundary lines?

Do you have any other boundaries in striving to live in purity?

Would you say that you have abusive tendencies?

Have you ever been abused mentally, physically or sexually?

What are your thoughts on pre-marital/post-marital counseling?

Do you have any obsessions?

Do you arrive to places on time?

Would you describe yourself as content or restless?

Are you a private person? Do you keep your feelings inside?

Do you like to be alone sometimes?

Do you have any major life regrets?

Name some of your proudest accomplishments.

Would you consider yourself more supportive or competitive?

Do you feel confident in yourself or are you constantly looking for the approval of others?

How do you react when an inappropriately dressed woman walks by?

AMBER GALLAGHER

Conflict Resolution

Do you have the ability to communicate and compromise for the benefit of all?

Do you tend to be quiet or speak your mind?

Do you think it is okay to yell when having a conflict?

Do you think that it is okay to use physical force while having a conflict?

Do you think that it is okay to go to sleep angry with your spouse?

What do you usually do when you are really angry with someone?

How was conflict resolved in the household you grew up in?

Do you have a positive way of dealing with anger? Have you ever walked off in your anger?

Do you hold grudges?

What do you think about the statement: "Sometimes you win the battle, but you lose the war."

Are you willing to listen to another side of the situation even when you do not agree?

Would you consider yourself tactful or brutally honest?

What would you do if your wife disagreed with how you were handling a situation?

Do think that it is okay for a couple to fight in front of others? In front of children?

Where should conflicts take place?

Have you ever studied, read books or attended conferences about effective communication? Would you be willing to?

Goals

Where do you see yourself in 5 years? In 10 years? In 25 years?

To where do you dream of traveling?

What is one thing you have always wanted to do?

Are you expecting a major life change in your future?

Job/Career

Do you feel settled and content in your current job?

What is your dream job?

What are some things about your job/career that you like? Dislike?

Hobbies/Free Time

How do you like to spend your free time?

How much time do you spend right now on your hobbies?

How much time will you spend participating in your hobbies once you are married?

AMBER GALLAGHER

What do you wish you had more time to do?

Do you have any dangerous hobbies?

For Fun

Do you like surprises?

What is your favorite color?

What is your favorite ice cream flavor?

What is your favorite movie?

What is your favorite type of food? Favorite restaurant?

What is your favorite date?

What is your favorite vacation spot?

What are your top ten most prized treasures?

Who do you look up to?

Do you like to travel? Where are your favorite places to go?

Who has the most influence in your life?

What are your favorite books to read?

18

Hearing God's Voice

Then he said: 'The God of our fathers has chosen you to know his will and to see the Righteous One and to hear words from his mouth. (Acts 22:14 NIV 1984)

The LORD confides in those who fear him; he makes his covenant known to them. (Psalm 25:14 NIV 1984)

In order to follow the Lord and make godly decisions about our relationships, careers, and other life choices, we need to hear from God. We need His direction, counsel, and comfort throughout our entire lives and Scripture lets us know that God has given us His Holy Spirit to do just that. We know that we have been given God's Holy Spirit for comfort and guidance. He will tell us things that we cannot possibly know. He will teach us the mysteries of God (John 14:26, 1 Corinthians 2:7-10). Then, how do we go about hearing from God? Does He speak audibly to us? What does His voice sound like? How do we distinguish His voice from all other voices that we hear?

There are definite ways and means that God has used to speak to people throughout time, and since He is the same God who does not change (Malachi 3:6) we will start by observing how He has spoken to those in past times.

AMBER GALLAGHER

What Does God's Voice Sound Like?

The Bible clearly gives us examples and even descriptions of God's voice from those who heard His sound audibly:

[Jesus prayed,] 'Father, glorify your name!' Then a voice came from heaven, 'I have glorified it, and will glorify it again.' The crowd that was there and heard it said it had thundered; others said an angel had spoken to him. Jesus said, 'This voice was for your benefit, not mine.' (John 12:28 NIV)

Sing to God, O kingdoms of the earth; sing praise to the Lord, Selah. To him who rides the ancient skies above, who thunders with mighty voice. (Psalm 68:32-33 NIV 1984)

His feet were like bronze glowing in a furnace, and his voice was like the sound of rushing waters. (Revelation 1:15 NIV 1984)

'Go out and stand before me on the mountain,' the Lord told him. And as Elijah stood there, the Lord passed by, and a mighty windstorm hit the mountain. It was such a terrible blast that the rocks were torn loose, but the Lord was not in the wind. After the wind there was an earthquake, but the Lord was not in the earthquake. [12] *And after the earthquake there was a fire, but the Lord was not in the fire.* [13] *And after the fire there was the sound of a gentle whisper.* (1 Kings 19:11-13 NLT)

I have never experienced hearing God's audible voice but rather I have sensed a thought or phrase—an impression of Him speaking to me in what is usually a peaceful and authoritative tone. I have heard gentle whispers, "Amber, I love you." or a nudging in my heart, "Amber, pray with her. Tell her I love her."

In What Other Ways Does God Speak to Us?

Scripture gives us instances of God using a variety of methods in order to speak to His people. At times, God used His Word, prophets, angels, dreams, and visions to relay His message.

His Word

All Scripture is inspired by God and is useful to teach us what is true and to make us realize what is wrong in our lives. It corrects us when we are wrong and teaches us to do what is right. (2 Timothy 3:16 NLT)

Such things were written in the Scriptures long ago to teach us. And the Scriptures give us hope and encouragement as we wait patiently for God's promises to be fulfilled. (Romans 15:4 NLT)

The Bible is God's Word given to us. He inspired men to write down His thoughts and His laws, as well as stories that depict His character and love toward His people. Many of the stories will depict characters that symbolize God such as the story of Abraham willing to lay down the life of his only son (Genesis 22). If you want to know God, then know His Word because it is there that you will find His heart toward you.

Dreams and Visions

'In the last days,' God says, 'I will pour out my Spirit on all people. Your sons and daughters will prophesy, your young men will see visions, your old men will dream dreams.' (Acts 2:17 NIV 1984)

In a dream, in a vision of the night, when deep sleep falls on men as they slumber in their beds, he may speak in their ears and terrify them with warnings, to turn man from wrongdoing and keep him from pride, to preserve his soul from the pit, his life from perishing by the sword. (Job 33:15-18 NIV 1984)

God spoke to several individuals such as Daniel, Isaiah, and Paul in the form of dreams and visions and the Scripture declares that we too can find God's direction at times through these methods (Joel 2:28).

A Dance with Jesus

I saw what looked like one of those grand ballrooms right out of the book *Pride and Prejudice*. Everything was made of dark, rich wood. Elegant candle-lit sconces graced the walls on every side and a crystal chandelier hung in a magnificent display from the center of the room's cathedral ceiling.

I was arrayed in a beautiful white ball gown as I danced in the arms of Jesus. My face was buried in His chest as if I wanted to escape the world around me. I couldn't help but notice how tightly He was holding me. We glided around the room to a silent melody.

Then, as my face rose to meet His gaze, I questioned, "Lord, is it time?"

Is it time for what? Ah! That's just it. That small question could have referred to any number of things, but looking in on this vision, I knew that I was asking for Jesus to fulfill the dreams that had long been hidden in my heart.

He said, "No, not yet. I just want to dance with you for a little while."

Again, I went back to burying my head into to His chest and He continued to wrap His arms all the way around me as we danced on. After a time, I questioned again, "Lord, is it time?"

"Yes, it's time," He pronounced with purpose beyond what I could understand in the moment.

He took me by the hand and we walked to the end of the ballroom where there were two massive, ornate wooden doors. When the doors opened as if by an invisible hand, all I could see was a brilliant light spilling into the room, illuminating everything in its path.

Searching for Happily-Ever-After

The Lord and I walked into the light and I knew He was taking me toward something truly amazing. I could feel the excitement of it swelling in my heart causing my pulse to quicken. The dreams and promises were to be fulfilled at last.

The room was left empty like a wedding whose bride and groom had departed. That's when I saw her—a little girl not more than five or six years old standing in the middle of the dance floor. She'd been watching with wild excitement as the couple had waltzed all around her. Those little eyes looked out from a face that resembled a younger version of my own. I noticed that she was garbed in a ragged little dress. I watched as her smile turned upside down when she realized she was left standing all alone.

This little girl's joy turned to what looked like fear as she realized that she was not going through those doors into the light with Jesus.

I felt such an ache as this little girl released a most pathetic cry, "I want to go too!" It was barely heard.

In an instant, Jesus appeared and with such tenderness in His voice said, "Oh, you are going too!"

He scooped this little child up in His strong arms and carried her through those big beautiful doors. Looking back on the abandoned ballroom, the little girl sighed, "That was so hard!"

Then the scene disappeared as quickly as it came.

This was a vision I had once during a time of intense prayer. Unbeknownst to me, it was right before one of the most difficult trials of my life. On my way home that night from church service and this amazing encounter with Jesus, I kept rehearsing the details of what I had seen in the vision. All the while, an old song called "The Dance" by Garth Brooks played in my mind like a soundtrack to my thoughts. I considered it odd because I hadn't heard this song since high school. I began to sing through the chorus when I came to the line, "I could've missed the pain, but I'd've had to miss the dance." I started to cry. I told the Lord that night how thankful I was for the trials and the pain in my life that had caused me to sit at His feet and find comfort in His arms.

I wrote this vision down and referred to it many times. I even tried to make it fit particular circumstances so that I could hope certain events would work out the way I wanted them to. I found out all too quickly that this would not do. My friend, Debbie, would say that is like "trying to make combat boots fit with an evening gown. No matter how hard you try, it simply doesn't go." It wasn't until I had gone through two failed and emotionally draining relationships that this vision made sense.

A few years later, when I sought out counseling, many of my "sessions" had to do with "little girl hurts" that I had carried throughout the years. I faced many paralyzing lies about fear, rejection, abandonment, love, self-esteem, and perfectionism that I had previously considered simply part of my life. I had to get back inside of that little girl heart that still exists in me and ask Jesus to show me His truth. It was a hard process and yet an absolutely freeing one. I could tell a change in my thought patterns as well as different reactions toward certain people and situations rather immediately once I had His truth in my heart.

Whew! That *was* hard, but that little girl heart is fully alive in me. At times, I will still go to the Lord if something seems to really affect me and I'll tell Him how I feel and ask Him to reveal His truth. God's truth is a powerful weapon that illuminates a situation or a memory and the devil's lies are rendered useless against us any longer.

I can say that this is one of the most powerful encounters I have had while walking with the Lord. He was speaking to me and He sure got my attention. I know I had severe heart pain that would have definitely interfered with me being able to handle and enjoy the promises that God wanted for my life. He simply went on in and healed me. It was time.

It may be that there is a work the Lord would like to accomplish in you before He takes you through open doors He has arranged for you. It may be beneficial to revisit the activity, *Discovering God's Truth* in Chapter Thirteen and if God speaks to you whether through visions, dreams, or any other way, then write it down and watch to see how He will use it to show you great and marvelous things.

Prophets and Angels (Ministers and Messengers)

If anyone speaks, he should do it as one speaking the very words of God. If anyone serves, he should do it with the strength God provides, so that in all things God may be praised through Jesus Christ. To him be the glory and the power forever and ever. Amen. (1 Peter 4:11 NIV 1984)

God used ministers called Prophets to proclaim His will and truth. The term "prophet" comes from the Hebrew word *nabi* which means "to utter" and an individual referred to as a prophet, would be one who serves as a channel of communication between God and men.[1] For instance, God sent a man named Jonah to proclaim to the city of Ninevah that if the people did not repent they would be destroyed. (See Jonah 3.)

The Lord also sent angels as messengers to proclaim to people the word and will of God. For example, the angels announced Jesus' birth to some shepherds and the angel, Gabriel, was sent to Mary to tell her she would give birth to Jesus (Luke 1:26-36, 2:8-14). Their mission was to proclaim truth—the words of God.

These days, God may use prophets, pastors, teachers, and mentors to speak a word of truth, direction or warning. If someone speaks to you about your life and direction or shares what they believe to be a word from God, how do you know it is really God? Consider the source. Is the person speaking into your life credible? Do they have evidence in their lives of one who humbly walks with God? Does this word line up with the teachings of the Bible? If not, reject the word immediately. Also, the Bible says that in order to test to see if a word is from the Lord, we must watch to see if it comes to pass. In the last days, many will claim to have a word from God, but some will be "wolves in sheep's clothing" trying to lead believers away from the Truth and away from God. The Bible refers to these individuals as "false prophets" (Matthew 7:15-17).

Look to God's instructions and teachings! People who contradict his word are completely in the dark. (Isaiah 8:20 NLT)

But the prophet who prophesies peace will be recognized as one truly sent by the Lord only if his prediction comes true. (Jeremiah 28:9 NIV 1984)

If what a prophet proclaims in the name of the Lord does not take place or come true, that is a message the Lord has not spoken. That prophet has spoken presumptuously. Do not be afraid of him. (Deuteronomy 18:22 ESV)

If you want to know if a thought is from God, test the fruit of it.

-Oswald Chambers

The Truth about Hearing from God

According to Scripture, there are certain truths we know about hearing from God.

Truth One: Those who follow God know His voice.

The man who enters by the gate is the shepherd of his sheep. The watchman opens the gate for him, and the sheep listen to his voice. He calls his own sheep by name and leads them out. When he has brought out all his own, he goes on ahead of them, and his sheep follow him because they know his voice. But they will never follow a stranger; in fact, they will run away from him because they do not recognize a stranger's voice. (John 10:2-5 NIV)

My sheep listen to my voice; I know them, and they follow me. (John 10:27 NIV 1984)

Think of it like this: If you've only recently met someone and they were to call, you may not recognize their voice or know their character. However, the more you get to know a person and even become friends, you will immediately recognize that this is the voice of someone you know and trust. They no longer have to tell you who they are before beginning a conversation, you already know because you are familiar with the sound of their voice and the character behind their words.

Truth Two: The Lord will never tell you to do something that goes against His Word.

. . . Evildoers and impostors will go from bad to worse, deceiving and being deceived. But as for you, continue in what you have learned and have become convinced of, because you know those from whom you learned it and how from infancy you have known the Holy Scriptures, which are able to make you wise for salvation through faith in Christ Jesus. (2 Timothy 3:13-15 NIV)

God is the same yesterday, today, and forever (Hebrews 13:8). That means His character is not going to change. I encourage you to check your motives as well as what the Word says before believing or acting on a thought or idea. Remember that when in doubt—wait!

Truth Three: God's voice does not cause confusion or panic.

For God is not the author of confusion, but of peace. (1 Corinthians 14:33a KJV)

Sometime before I was married, I began to hang out with a new group of friends who had recently begun attending our church. Early on, one of the girls began to bring to my attention a certain young man pretty frequently. She and her husband would have this guy show up almost every time I would be over at their house. I started to feel a lot of pressure to "date" this guy. He was a great guy—cute, smart, talented, but I felt a check in my heart. I began to pray about it and ask the Lord to direct me. The guy eventually approached me about starting a romantic relationship. I told him I was only interested in being friends and getting to know him. He continued to pursue. About three months into the friendship, several of us went to a "game night" at this guy's house. During one of the games, I felt a strong impression. I heard the word, "NO!" in my mind. It was so forceful that I flinched there at my seat. I don't know to this day if anyone caught that interchange, but I was certain the Lord was giving me direction. Later that week, I was able to have a conversation where I told the guy that I felt a romantic relationship was not the Lord's will for us and I knew we would never be more than friends. The guy seemed relieved and said that he had actually been feeling the same direction in his heart. Although some in the crowd were disappointed, I knew this was right and felt completely peaceful about the decision. The guy and I were able to remain friends within the bounds of this group, but a romance was never made.

If you are feeling confusion or uncertainty, I would recommend that you wait before acting and continue talking it over with the Lord in prayer. The Lord will ultimately give clarity in the situation. It could be that your lack of peace is God's cue to you.

Truth Four: God's voice guides in authority, wisdom, patience, and peace while the enemy's voice discourages by pressuring, pushing, accusing, and condemning.

Do not be anxious about anything, but in everything, by prayer and petition, with thanksgiving, present your requests to God. And the peace, which transcends all understanding, will guard your hearts and minds in Christ Jesus. (Philippians 4:6-7 NIV 1984)

I went one weekend to an event on a particular college campus with my church youth group. I was already attending a different college close to home, but on the day we were to leave on this trip, I heard this nagging voice say over and again, "You will transfer and go to this college." It immediately did not set right with my spirit. I did not have peace. As a matter of fact, I felt really confused, anxious, and heavy. I felt pushed to make a decision. I talked to my youth pastor on the way home and told him how I felt. He agreed that the voice of God would not pressure, confuse or cause despair. Instead, His voice brings clarity, peace, and assurance. I finally said, "Lord, if you want me to move, I will. However I refuse to take one step without knowing that this is definitely You. I will wait to see if your peace comes because Lord, You know I am willing to follow You."

After I waited, the pressuring stopped. The heaviness went away and I knew that voice had not come from God.

Truth Five: God will confirm His Word.

Then the disciples went out and preached everywhere, and the Lord worked with them and confirmed his word by the signs that accompanied it. (Mark 16:20 NIV 1984)

If you feel that the Lord has given you direction or a promise, keep it in your heart just as the Scripture says about Mary, the mother of Jesus: "Mary treasured up all these things and pondered them in her heart" (Luke 2:19 NIV). You may feel that this is a promise to be treasured between you and the Lord and at other times, it will perhaps be something you feel at liberty to share with others and have them pray with you. Look for encouragement and direction in the Scriptures and listen to counsel from trusted spiritual leaders and advisors.

Open and Closed Doors

I know all the things you do, and I have opened a door for you that no one can close. You have little strength, yet you obeyed my word and did not deny me. (Revelation 3:8 NLT)

I will give him the key to the house of David—the highest position in the royal court. When he opens doors, no one will be able to close them; when he closes doors, no one will be able to open them. (Isaiah 22:22 NLT)

I was contemplating getting engaged to a young man. We had looked at rings. Yet again, when I prayed about the relationship, I sensed that familiar uneasiness. Looking back, I realize that I should have stopped there, but I felt a lot of pressure from the guy and honestly from myself too. I didn't want to miss out on an opportunity because of fear. Here was a Christian man who loved God and wanted to go into ministry and he wanted to marry me. It was a really difficult time because I wanted to marry a godly man who had a heart for ministry. I talked with a friend and she said, "You can step in this direction and watch for the Lord to either keep the door open or close it in front of you." I kept stepping. There came a point in the relationship when he was going to leave for an extended mission trip, promising that when he got back, he was going to go talk to my father and ask permission to marry me. Right before he left, I started fasting and praying and continued the first few days that he was gone. Things seemed fine at first. Exactly one week after my fast ended, He called me. The conversation was uncomfortably strained and he said he was having serious doubts about our relationship. The last conversation we had that week was much of the same. Our phone call got cut off and the guy never called me again. I went through some serious unresolved heart issues because of what this event stirred in me, but I have to praise the Lord because He answered my prayer and abruptly closed the door.

It is essential to understand that every open door is not necessarily from God. Wait and remember that His plans will lead us toward Himself and not away. When *God* starts a thing, you can be sure that He will be faithful to see it through and when He closes a door, I encourage you not to pine for what you feel you have lost, but set your face forward and trust that He will amaze you with His plan if you'll continue to follow Him.

Being confident of this, that he who began a good work in you will carry it on to completion until the day of Christ Jesus. (Philippians 1:6 NIV 1984)

Also, keep in mind that even though God may have called you to a particular task, does not mean that He will never lead you in a different direction. In his book, *Alone With God: Biblical Inspiration for the Unmarried*, Michael Warden explains that:

You can always tell when the presence of God has moved on from a job or calling to which He originally led you. Everything that was once easy is suddenly burdensome and hard. Things that use to energize you now drain you to the dregs. 'But didn't God call me to do this?' you wonder. Yes, of course. But now He is calling you somewhere else. Once God's presence has moved on, you would do well not to hang around either, any longer than necessary, however settled you have become. Pack up your things, find out where God's Spirit is going, and follow Him there.[2]

It's a Process!

The ability to discern God's voice and follow His direction is a process. His will is not always the most obvious. I know there have been instances where God simply has wanted me to search Him out in a matter. When I need to hear from God, I must take the time to communicate and spend time with Him talking the thing over. I think He enjoys that fellowship with us immensely. Of course, I must always come back to a crucial piece of advice: Before making the decision to marry a particular man, I encourage you to spend time with your First Love, Jesus. Allow Him to have the necessary time with you all to Himself where He can teach you to hear and follow His voice.

You will seek Me and find Me when you search for Me with all your heart. (Jeremiah 29:13 NASB)

Whether you turn to the right or to the left, your ears will hear a voice behind you, saying 'This is the way; walk in it.' (Isaiah 30:21 NIV)

Once you are certain that God has spoken and directed you, then do the thing. Putting it off will only bring anxiety. Save yourself the angst and obey in what He is asking of you. Remember that delayed obedience is still disobedience.

Today when you hear his voice, don't harden your hearts as Israel did when they rebelled. (Hebrews 3:15b NLT)

The Wait

19

When Dreams Die

Surviving a Devastated Heart

The Way of Death

To desire is to open our heart to the possibility of pain; to shut down our hearts is to die altogether.

-John Eldredge, *The Journey of Desire*[1]

What happens when our dreams seem to die? When what we hoped and planned for is now gone? For some of you, this is a chapter that caught your attention because you have walked this road or maybe you are on it now. Until you have walked the way of death, it is hard to capture into words what this road is like. Have you ached to the point of physical pain over a promise that seemed to die right in front of your eyes? Have you asked the Lord, "Will I survive this?" Has it been painful to an extreme where you have stayed in bed asking God to take you now because being with Him is all the hope you seem to have left? Do you have to constantly pray through the day to survive? Are your family and coworkers tiptoeing around at a complete loss as to how to help you? What is the purpose? And of course the big question most of us have asked at some point, "Why, God?"

I have felt every one of those emotions and I imagine that so have some of you. We have generally all felt loss or been completely heartsick. Goodbyes are hard and death is painful.

In the same breath, I would have to say that through brokenness and times standing at the altar of sacrificed dreams, the Lord has shown me that there is beauty in death. He doesn't view it as we do. I don't think He sees death as final as we tend to view it. He even says things in His Word like "Precious in the sight of the LORD is the death of his faithful servants" (Psalm 116:15 NIV), or "Very truly I tell you, unless a kernel of wheat falls to the ground and dies, it remains only a single seed. But if it dies, it produces many seeds" (John 12:24 NIV).

I am always reminded of this "beauty in death" when I am out driving in October and November. I love autumn. It is actually my favorite season—the crisp air, apple cider slushies, farmer's markets, fall festivals, and the colorful trees. Sigh! This is why I live in Ohio.

I will admit that I do feel a twinge of sadness knowing that warmer days are behind us, but that is quickly replaced by an awe of all the colors in God's paint palette. The reason we are able to see the beautiful colors of the leaves in fall is because of a death that is taking place. Three things contribute to this death: lack of food supply, colder and harsher weather, and the lengthening of night. Once the leaves die, they are pushed out—a final pruning necessary for the tree to survive.[2] I am constantly amazed at how God teaches us His miraculous design through nature.

We are no different, you know. In the seeming death of our dreams, we experience a lack of what we have known as comfortable and normal to us. Often with this removal of something or someone who once brought sustenance to our heart, we become hungry for answers. The harshness of weathering the storm can feel like such a scary place because as we try to brave the tempest, we can at times lose sight of the direction in which we were once headed. Then of course, there is the lengthening of our night. Our hard times seem dark and we wonder when the light is going to shine again. When will we laugh and sing and dance again? Weeping truly does "endure" for the long night, but the Lord is quick to remind us that "joy comes in the morning." (See Psalm 30:5.) A new day will come and we find that we have not lost our smile after all. It was simply in hiding for a while. Keep in mind that just as the leaves of a tree, this winter season of pruning is necessary for us too. Otherwise, we may hang on a little too tightly to our fruitless ways, dead-end jobs or unhealthy relationships. God is the all-knowing Gardener. He is very aware of when and how much to prune from our lives. His loving and gracious Father's heart is wise to the fact that this is a necessary process for our survival.

A precious young woman told me her story of a heart-wrenching, difficult time she had endured—it was a death of sorts. Her husband left her after a year of marriage. This lady was served divorced papers without so much as a conversation or a "Goodbye, have a nice life!" It seemed that there was no hope, but oh you should've seen her. Often in church service, I would notice her feverishly writing down notes, drinking in every word. She would spend great amounts of time fasting and praying. Instead of turning her back on God because of her pain, she allowed the Lord to comfort her. I cannot forget every time she would smile through tears in the face of another bout of bad news and say, "Well, God is answering my prayers." Her life was marked by what the Bible describes as "joy unspeakable and full of glory." It is to the glory of God that a woman can survive what she has endured, but survive she did. Where is her smile? It never left her. Not because she was delivered out of her circumstance, which she now has been, but her smile was there because she was sustained and satisfied through her love affair with Christ. This is the kind of joy that a world who refuses relationship with Christ sadly cannot understand.

What Happens in Death?

If we yield to the process, we will be able to see something truly extraordinary happen in death:

God comes near to us.
We are healed.
We join Jesus in the fellowship of His suffering.
We gain crisp spiritual vision and hearing.
We can see the supernatural movement of God.
Those around us will be drawn to God.
We learn perseverance.

God Comes Near to Us

The Bible promises that "The LORD is close to the brokenhearted and saves those who are crushed in spirit" (Psalm 34:18 NIV 1984). Not only that, but the Bible says, "He heals the brokenhearted and binds up their wounds" (Psalm 147:3 NIV 1984).

The Good Samaritan

Jesus told a story of a Jewish man who was traveling. On his way to Jericho, he was mugged and beaten pretty badly. The robbers even left him to die on the side of the rode. Later on, a priest (pastor) walked by, saw the man, and refused to stop. Instead he moved to the opposite side of the rode as if the beaten man were not even there. Then, a Levite (a man who was "set apart for God") passed by and reacted in the same manner. A little later on, a Samaritan man walked by and stopped to help the man. That would have been highly unusual because Jews and Samaritans typically hated one another (John 4:9). However, the Samaritan had compassion on this helpless victim. He bandaged the man's wounds, put the broken man on his own donkey, and paid for him to not only stay at an inn, but also to receive treatment for his ailments (Luke 10:29-37).

This is a beautiful illustration of the compassion that Christ has shown to us. It was our sin that nailed Him to a cross and yet Jesus has compassion on us in *our* suffering. The Lord will never abandon us in our grief and brokenness. He is actually drawn to those who are suffering. He is well acquainted with loss, rejection, and sorrow and He longs to come near and bind up our wounds.

We Are Healed

My heart was broken . . . again. My plans of marriage and a family were gone. Heartache pressed so hard it was as if I could feel the chasm this divide had left in my heart. I couldn't sleep. I couldn't eat. The only thing that made any sense was to walk. For hours, I'd get up in the morning and trek up and down the long gravel road on my parents' farm. I'd try to talk to God, but words were too much. Mostly I would feel Him as a hovering Presence, silent, but present. I remembered how He had showed me a vision of us dancing. My head was buried in His chest and hadn't He said, "I'm coming for all of it"? He had come for my pain. That was good because it felt like every ounce of pain had erupted to the surface of my drowning heart.

The truth of the matter is that brokenness and sorrow are powerful tools. They oftentimes act as keys, opening doors to the deep and secret places of a person's heart. This allows the Lord access to come in and do the healing work. I personally found that brokenness loosened my grip on things to which I had previous clung for security. In the end, I was left holding onto the Lord alone.

On one of these walks, for a moment, I saw a picture of me walking this same road. Only this time my hands were raised in praise. A smile was etched across my face as tears of joy covered my cheeks. It was a picture of a future time that would eventually and gloriously come to pass, but for the present, I was called to walk through the pain into God's perfect work and I can say looking back, it was worth it.

Every gap in your life makes room for the Lover of your soul. God uses time to unwrap presents that appear as curses.

-Beth Moore, *James: Mercy Triumphs*[3]

Forgiveness

In my pain I found that one of the hurdles I had to conquer was that of forgiving someone whom I had trusted for the crushing blow they had delivered to my heart. I didn't know how to find closure and forgive a person who took no responsibility for having been hateful and cruel. It was perfectly clear that this individual whom I had previously cared deeply for and once enjoyed a flourishing relationship with had no intention of apologizing or making amends.

Several months later, I was at a weekend conference and had actually walked down to the altar to pray with a friend. The worship band was singing. I believe it was right in the middle of a song when the worship leader stopped and began to talk about forgiving those who have wronged us even when they will not take the responsibility for hurting us. I stopped and my eyes couldn't help but be transfixed. How did this man know? He went on to say, "I am sorry to you, I am so sorry!" He began to cry as he kept apologizing. Tears were streaming down my cheeks as I felt the Lord whisper to me, "Amber, right there is your 'I'm sorry.'"

True freedom comes through forgiveness. God can heal our wounds without the help and apologies of those who have hurt us. When we refuse to forgive, the person who suffers most is us. Unforgiveness will make a person hard, angry, and bitter, acting as a cancer to the mind and heart. When we forgive, our offender no longer has a hold on us. This doesn't mean that trust has to be given back to the person, but it does mean our heart is free from seeking vengeance. It is always best that vengeance be left to the Lord. After all, He knows precisely how to handle it (Romans 12:19).

We Join Jesus in the Fellowship of His Suffering

When we suffer in any way, we are able to experience a mere fraction of the suffering that Jesus endured. He was betrayed and treated cruelly. He was given punishment for crimes He never committed. He was despised and hated by those who were supposed to love and worship Him. He endured loss of reputation, family, friends, and even His life.

When you first meet someone, what draws you together? Do you not begin to bond when you find that you have something in common? How about when you are trying to minister to someone who is hurting, isn't it powerful to be able to say, "I've been where you are now . . . ?" When the Lord comes up next to the broken-hearted who has been betrayed and rejected and He says, "I'm sorry for your pain. I have been there too," that speaks to us. He is touched by our pain. It is familiar to Him. He, above anyone, knows how you feel and He stays by your side in the midst of your brokenness.

Another aspect of pain I have noticed is that every trial I can think of having encountered, has in some way offered opportunities to testify of the Lord's faithfulness to others who are broken around me. Most people feel really lonely in their pain, but something about hearing your story may give them courage to open up and allow you to speak hope into their lives.

Yes, we will join Jesus in the fellowship of His suffering, but, dear heart, we will in the end, also share in His marvelous glory.

The Spirit himself testifies with our spirit that we are God's children. [17]Now if we are children, then we are heirs—heirs of God and co-heirs with Christ, if indeed we share in his sufferings in order that we may also share in his glory. (Romans 8:16-17 NIV)

AMBER GALLAGHER

We Gain Crisp Spiritual Vision and Hearing

Have you ever noticed that when we experience pain, trivial concerns seem of much less concern and our priorities become all the more clear to us? We start wanting to spend our time more productively. We want to build stronger bonds in the relationships around us with people we dearly love.

My husband was so affected by the tragedy of the 9/11 events that he felt the need to say "I love you" as frequently as possible to his parents, siblings, and friends. He wanted to make sure that they always knew how he felt about them. It's a good thing, too, because a few years later he would lose his mother to cancer. If you ask him, Brian would say that yes, his mother's passing was extremely sad; however, she went to Heaven knowing that she was loved. "There was nothing left unsaid," he will tell you.

My father-in-law, Wayne, makes every effort to encourage the husbands and wives around him to cherish their time together and to love each other as fully as possible while they have the precious opportunity to do so. I once heard a man comment on how nice it was to have the bed to himself while his wife was away on business. I immediately looked at my father-in-law and sure enough I heard him say, "[Having the bed to yourself] is not all it's cracked up to be."

My husband and I have a keen awareness of not wanting to miss out on loving each other with our actions and words for one single day. We know first-hand that time is short here on this planet and therefore, we are determined to make our time count.

We Can See the Supernatural Movement of God

Take a look at the story of Mary, Martha, and Lazarus in John 11:1-15 (NLT):

A man named Lazarus was sick. He lived in Bethany with his sisters, Mary and Martha. ²This is the Mary who later poured the expensive perfume on the Lord's feet and wiped them with her hair. Her brother,

Lazarus, was sick. ³*So the two sisters sent a message to Jesus telling him, 'Lord, your dear friend is very sick.'*

⁴*But when Jesus heard about it he said, 'Lazarus' sickness will not end in death. No, it happened for the glory of God so that the Son of God will receive glory from this.' ⁵So although Jesus loved Martha, Mary, and Lazarus, ⁶he stayed where he was for the next two days. ⁷Finally, he said to his disciples, 'Let's go back to Judea.'*

⁸*But his disciples objected. 'Rabbi,' they said, 'only a few days ago the people in Judea were trying to stone you. Are you going there again?'*

⁹*Jesus replied, 'There are twelve hours of daylight every day. During the day people can walk safely. They can see because they have the light of this world. ¹⁰But at night there is danger of stumbling because they have no light.' ¹¹Then he said, 'Our friend Lazarus has fallen asleep, but now I will go and wake him up.'*

¹²*The disciples said, 'Lord, if he is sleeping, he will soon get better!' ¹³They thought Jesus meant Lazarus was simply sleeping, but Jesus meant Lazarus had died.*

¹⁴*So he told them plainly, 'Lazarus is dead. ¹⁵And for your sakes, I'm glad I wasn't there, for now you will really believe. Come, let's go see him.'*

If you read the rest of the story, you will find that Jesus comes on the scene and raises Lazarus from the dead, a supernatural act of God. I'm not necessarily saying that God will raise someone from the dead, although He is quite capable of doing so, but there will be a supernatural work done by God in the midst of our losses.

A young man who previously attended our youth group had an accident in which he fell and hit his head on the cement ground and died. It was such a sad funeral and yet, hundreds of students and some of his family members for whom he had prayed were saved that day.

Have you considered that it may be in the death of a relationship, you may be healed or even rescued from a "disaster waiting to happen." Much we do not understand, but if we keep our eyes on God and our hand firmly clasped in His, He will lead us through and allow our eyes to see His supernatural power at work so that the "Son of God will receive glory from this" (John 11:4).

Those Around Us Will Be Drawn to God

Check out the outcome in this story of Paul and Silas (Acts 16:22-26 NIV):

The crowd joined in the attack against Paul and Silas, and the magistrates ordered them to be stripped and beaten with rods. ²³*After they had been severely flogged, they were thrown into prison, and the jailer was commanded to guard them carefully.* ²⁴*When he received these orders, he put them in the inner cell and fastened their feet in the stocks.*

²⁵*About midnight Paul and Silas were praying and singing hymns to God, and the other prisoners were listening to them.* ²⁶*Suddenly there was such a violent earthquake that the foundations of the prison were shaken. At once all the prison doors flew open, and everyone's chains came loose.*

Paul and Silas were ministers of the gospel. They were trying to bring the good news of Christ to the people. Yet, after they had commanded an evil spirit to come out of a fortune-telling girl, her masters incited the crowd against Paul and Silas, which landed them in prison. What betrayal and loss they endured. How would they ever fulfill their callings to minister now? Instead of despairing, Paul and Silas sang hymns of praise to the Lord in their cell while the other prisoners were listening. Then, God sent an earthquake to open the prison doors and rattle their chains loose. If you look closely, Paul and Silas were not the only ones who were freed that night. It says that *all* the prison doors flew open and *everyone's* chains came loose (v. 26).

When we go through loss, know that others are watching to see how we respond. When we praise the Lord in spite of what we have lost or suffered, refusing to give up but choosing instead to trust, not only will we be freed, but those watching us will come to the knowledge of a powerful, life-saving God and they too will be set free.

We Learn Perseverance

Consider it pure joy, my brothers, whenever you face trials of many kinds, ³because you know that the testing of your faith develops perseverance. ⁴Perseverence must finish its work so that you may be mature and complete, not lacking anything. (James 1:2-4 NIV)

The truth is that suffering reminds us that we are not quite home yet. We live in a fallen world and suffering causes us to look up and place our hope in God rather than in ourselves, our plans or our circumstances. Treasure is found in the dark trials we face. One of those treasures is perseverance—to walk steadily on when we feel like giving up. Perseverance produces maturity and a strength we never knew we could possess. As the old saying goes, "When God is all you have, you realize that He is all you need." One day, we will see much more clearly. We will understand how near God came to us through it all. We were never abandoned. On the contrary, He taught us how to grow, mature, and persevere.

In her book, *Lies Women Believe and the Truth That Sets them Free*, Nancy Leigh Demoss captures a truly meaningful explanation for suffering: "All suffering is purposeful and intentional. [God] knows exactly the intensity and the duration that are needed to fulfill His purposes. He will not allow our suffering to last any longer or to be any more severe than is necessary to accomplish His will."[4]

If we could only see what He sees and know what He knows, but alas we do not and so we must trust His heart even when we cannot see His hands moving in our lives. We must remind ourselves if need be, that God will keep His promise to work "for the good of those who love him, who have been called according to his purpose" (Romans 8:28 NIV).

Letting Go

Hope deferred makes the heart sick, but a longing fulfilled is a tree of life. (Proverbs 13:12 NIV)

Even if you've ached over a desired dream, the safest thing you can do is let it go into God's hands.

Stormie Omartian writes in her book, *Just Enough Light for the Step I'm On: Trusting God in the Tough Times*, "When the Lord gives you a promise; you will probably have to lay it down to the point of death."[5] I have certainly found this to be true in my life. Once, on one of my walks down that old gravel lane on my parents' farm, I built a little stone altar and there standing symbolically as in ancient times, I placed my dreams of a husband, children, and ministry on that altar and allowed them to die. I told the Lord that I would love Him no matter what. It was hard, but I was broken and too sad to carry them with me anyway. I told Him that whatever may come, I knew He would help me to survive it and that I loved Him and would never walk away from Him and I meant it.

Some of the dreams stayed dead. I can look back on them in the light of where God has me now and truly say that I am grateful that God did not give me those things for which I had asked. He gave me new dreams that were better than the old ones, which were limited and powerless. Other dreams God resurrected and they resurfaced in my life more powerful than ever before. He has shown me time and again that He does not forget anything we have committed into His hands.

If you are in the valley of the shadow of death, dear friend, keep holding on! Keep walking until you get to the part where He causes you to lay down in green pastures beside still waters. (See Psalm 23.) The ache will fade; hope will fill your heart again and the redemptive work will be done. Press on and know this—pain is never wasted.

20

When the Wait Is Hard

Sowing and Reaping

Those who sow in tears will reap with songs of joy. (Psalm 126:5 NIV)

I have heard many ladies-in-waiting tell their stories. Without fail, these precious young women will lament at how often they struggle. It is no doubt difficult at times, especially during holidays, weddings, and funerals. Can you relate?

I decided to read through my old journals. I wanted to remember the highs and lows of my journey as I was preparing to write this book. Some days I loved the freedom and adventure of being single, and other days I longed to be held by my future husband or to hold my own babies.

Reading through those journals was entertaining and also a little exhausting. My heart went out to my parents who had to watch me go through my heartache and woes. I ached to come alongside that Amber girl to encourage and to rescue her. I imagine that God felt that way too when the story was unfolding. While I was walking through the journey, I didn't quite have the perspective that I do now reading about it after the story has now been played out in many ways. I wasn't worried this time around about where the story was headed because I have seen the end of this chapter. God knew that one day I would see the harvest from the tears and the waiting. From this perspective, I felt myself silently cheering, "Keep going, Amber girl. It's not over yet! Wait until you see how this one ends. It's going to end well!" Oh yes, I now know that it was worthwhile to walk onward through the ache endured in the wait as it was purposeful in leading this lady straight into the destiny God had planned. We, myself included, instinctively prefer to take the road less painful, but it would do us well to remember that the "waiting pain" is a burn altogether different than that caused by taking matters into our own hands, which draws the sojourner down a road fraught with unnecessary agony.

It is such a comforting thought to know that my days were written about long before one of them came to be (Psalm 139:16). No, God wasn't worried either watching my story play out because He knew exactly where He was taking me. I walked away from this sentimental journey more grateful than ever for God's plans to heal, deliver, and guide my life.

Remember His Promises

When you feel like the Lord has given you promises in life, one of the most difficult things to do is to wait for them to come to pass. Sometimes, our eyes shift to our circumstances and we simply forget. This is another reason why I strongly recommend journaling your prayers and promises. When I have distanced myself from God's promises, I can become lonely, bitter, dissatisfied, and begin to question God: "Lord, why does everyone else get to have a husband? Will I ever be able to have children? Why do doors seem to be opening for others while I am still doing the same old things?"

In my self-pity, I have compared myself to young David, who was kept back in the fields alone herding the sheep while his brothers were presented favor, opportunities, and meetings with famous prophets. Talk about feeling passed over and left out.

I realized that it is not up to me or others to make things happen for me. All of David's brothers may have been given consideration for kingship, but it was the Lord who would pull David out of the pasture and set him in the palace.

God is no different now than He was then. If He has something in mind for you, then you may be sure that He will not stop until the thing is accomplished.

As the rain and the snow come down from heaven, and do not return to it without watering the earth and making it bud and flourish, so that it yields seed for the sower and bread for the eater, [11]*so is my word that goes out from my mouth: It will not return to me empty, but will accomplish what I desire and achieve the purpose for which I sent it.* (Isaiah 55:10-11 NIV 1984)

When I go through the lonely times, I have to deliberately push the pause button and get back into His Word. I'll pull out my Bible and ask God to speak to me again to remind me of His plans and He will. One such time, several years ago, I needed His encouragement. The Lord caused the following verses to jump off of the page at me and I would think of them often:

Lift up your eyes all around, and see: They all gather together, they come to you; Your sons shall come from afar, And your daughters shall be nursed at your side. [5]*Then you shall see and become radiant, And your heart shall swell with joy; Because the abundance of the sea shall be turned to you.*

[20]*And the days of your mourning shall be ended.*

[22]*I, the Lord, will hasten it in its time.* (Isaiah 60: 4-5a, 20b, 22b NJKV)

With that said, I'd like to be open and share with you several entries from my old journals. You will read about some hard and lonely as well as happy and exciting parts of my story. In doing so, I hope that you will allow me to commune with you if you are suffering and encourage you if you are in doubt. I pray that God will help you to set your face like a "flint" determined to believe and hope your way all the way to your own "Promised Land" (Isaiah 50:7). It's going to be worth it! Who knows? When it's all said and done, maybe you too will need to share your story with someone. They will need to know your "Once Upon a Time" tale.

This is my journey of sowing and reaping . . .

21

Sowing Seeds

January 18, 1995 to January 27, 2003

1/18/95 Amber age 16

I am now in eleventh grade . . . sixteen and I finally got my license. My dream is to become a country singer. I have decided 'boys will be boys.' Will they ever grow out of this stage? I do not have a boyfriend and haven't for my whole high school career. For now, I am content. I have not had sex yet, nor do I plan to until marriage. People respect me for it and I like that. It's very hard to find a good Christian guy, but still I rest assured knowing God has my husband already chosen. I pray for him every day, and I feel a certain kind of love for him. Is that weird? Loving someone you do not know? I hope we will be all that each of us has ever dreamed of having . . . another one for God. What a struggle sometimes.

3/18/95

I feel like life has flown by. It seems like yesterday that I was learning to ride a bike, tie my shoes, and wear make-up. I've asked the Lord to guide me and I know He will. I'm thankful that He will never leave me. This boy likes me. He is cute, but he has had a bit of a reputation. Could he forego all of his physical desires just to be with me? I've made up my mind to tell him straight out that I don't believe in 'such things'... before marriage anyway.

10/3/99 Amber age 21

The Lord is the only strength I have. If not for Him my heart would not have survived this. I fell pretty hard. Now I'm dusting myself off and trying to move on, but sometimes I feel so weak and frail. Oh God, be my portion.

12/2/99

'For I know the plans I have for you,' declares the LORD, 'plans to prosper you and not to harm you, plans to give you hope and a future.' (Jeremiah 29:11 NIV)

1/30/00

Lord, I love You. I want Your perfect will in my life.

2/6/00

The Lord keeps reminding me, 'Remember your First Love.'

2/13/00

For a while now, I've been concerned with God's calling on my life—not knowing exactly what that is... what I should do or where I should go. Jesus' ministry started when he was thirty and meanwhile He worked as a carpenter; now He is using His carpentry skills to build mansions for those who give their hearts to Him.

'My Father's house has many rooms; if that were not so, would I have told you that I am going there to prepare a place for you?³ And if I go and *prepare a place for you, I will come back and take you to be with me that you also may be where I am. ⁴You know the way to the place where I am going.'* (John 14:2-4 NLT)

7/1/00

Helen Watkins, our pastor's wife, passed away last Friday, June twenty-third. It has been a very sad time. Not only has our pastor's wife passed, but it's like the love affair with Jack and Helen is completed. I felt like I was a part of this beautiful love story. I can't even count the number of times he [Pastor] told us about how he saved her from drowning in that river. He became exhausted struggling and decided he would give in and die with her. It was in that instant they were saved. When she died on Friday, he told her, 'This looks like a river I'm not going to be able to get you out of.' I believe that their love affair was and will be a legacy that I will even tell my children about. The Lord spoke to me Thursday night of camp that He wants our love affair to be a legacy. How awesome!

7/3/00

Our youth pastor wants me to take over leading the praise team. It's scary. Lord, give me strength.

9/4/00 Amber age 22

I wonder . . . will the day ever come when I will stand in the midst of the purpose—the assignment, and will I say, 'This is what it all has been for'?

5/24/01

I keep feeling like there is something more. I feel in every area of my life I am waiting and not having a clue as to what will unfold. I'm really searching. I feel overwhelmed at times.

AMBER GALLAGHER

8/30/01 Amber age 23

I feel like I am being pruned. Lord, you are in control. Take away everything that hinders my relationship with You; carry me through, my Faithful Prince.

10/30/01

I have surrendered the pen of my life over to the Author and Finisher of my faith to write my love story.

5/2/02

The Lord has really been speaking to me about His love and how He feels about His bride.

'Romance is the deepest thing in life; it is deeper even than reality. Our heart is made for a great drama, because it is the reflection of the Author of that story.'

-Brent Curtis and John Eldredge, *The Sacred Romance*[1]

7/15/02

I love you, my Prince of Peace. You alone complete me. I trust in You. You are my Portion forever.

8/30/02 Amber age 24

[My last night in Paris, France]. We went to the Louvre and watched the sun go down. A man was playing 'Yesterday' on his violin. The Lord was with me. I know you were, Lord.

10/19/02

I feel as if I have gone through a death. I have been broken, but He is close to those who have a 'broken heart and a crushed spirit' (Psalm 34:8).

'Beauty helps when we grieve. There is a freedom in grief."

-John Eldredge, The Journey of Desire[2]

10/25/02

God is faithful. He is restoring me. I have been called to a rest. I am noticing beauty all around me.

1/27/03

I can feel Your design everywhere. It almost overwhelms me. I want to run ahead, but I dare not lest I fall.

22

The Rain

August 9, 2003 to June 13, 2006

8/9/03 Amber age 25

Lord, I want to know Your will for me. Thank you, Lord, that You never break my heart. You are the greatest Love this heart has ever and will ever know. Thank you for our walks where the whole world is silent and it's simply You and me.

4/17/04

Lord, speak to me again. Your voice is the only voice I want to hear.

4/18/04

[I felt the Lord say to me]:

'I am so proud of you, My little girl. I have guided every step. I will heal your wounds. I will dry your tears. I will sit with you and tell you all that you are to Me.'

AMBER GALLAGHER

9/19/04 Amber age 26

Lord, I find myself longing for a family today. I want to have children. I want to have a home. Lord, I pray that you would speak to my husband on my behalf. Help me to 'be all here' right now.

9/29/04

Lord, when will it stop hurting? I know you have a plan. Guard this heart . . . even from me.

10/7/04

Lord, You tell me of a time when You'll take away the pain, wipe every tear away. You tell me that you keep all these tears in a bottle set aside for me—that You are still the King of all I can't see.

10/18/04

I will guide you in the way of wisdom and lead you along straight paths. When you walk, your steps will not be hampered; when you run, you will not stumble. Hold on to instruction, do not let it go; guard it well for it is your life. (Proverbs 4:11-13 NIV)

Oh, Lord, may it be so for this life. Sometimes I feel like I know the way to go and other times I feel so lost.

10/23/04

I believe the Lord has given me these verses as promises. They are the 'Balm of Gilead' that I have desperately needed. Thank you, my beautiful Savior.

'As for me, this is my covenant with them,' says the LORD. 'My Spirit, who is on you, and my words that I have put in your mouth will not depart from your mouth, or from the mouths of your children, or from the

mouths of their descendants from this time on and forever,' says the LORD. (Isaiah 59:21 NIV)

See, darkness covers the earth and thick darkness is over the peoples, but the LORD rises upon you and his glory appears over you. Lift up your eyes and look about you: All assemble and come to you; your sons come from afar, and your daughters are carried on the hip. (Isaiah 60:2, 4 NIV)

10/24/04

Lord, You are my Kinsman Redeemer. I am eternally bound to You, my Maker and my Husband. Your words satisfy me more completely than anything else ever could. I love you, Lord.

No one who hopes in you will ever be put to shame. ⁴Show me your ways, LORD, teach me your paths. ⁵Guide me in your truth and teach me, for you are God my Savior, and my hope is in you all day long. ⁶Remember, LORD, your great mercy and love, for they are from of old. (Psalm 25:3a, 4-6 NIV)

Instead of your shame you will receive a double portion, and instead of disgrace you will rejoice in your inheritance. And so you will inherit a double portion in your land, and everlasting joy will be yours. (Isaiah 61:7 NIV)

11/14/04

Lord, I have felt Your strong hands holding me today. I know there is not one thing I can do to change my situation. It all belongs to You. I have felt Your peace. I saw Your rainbow today. I was reminded that it is the sign of Your promise.

For He spoke, and it was done. He commanded, and it stood fast. (Psalm 33:9 NKJV)

'I make all things new.' (Revelation 21:5 NKJV)

AMBER GALLAGHER

11/28/04

'Going through a waiting period doesn't mean that there is nothing happening, because when you are waiting on the Lord, He is always moving in your life.'

-Stormie Omartian, *Just Enough Light for the Step I'm On*[1]

12/8/04

The place I feel safe is right here—shut away in my room writing in this journal. Oh God, that I were a dove and could fly away and rest.

Lord, I want a man of honor and unwavering integrity. A man who is mature and ready. A man who makes me laugh hysterically. A man who can speak his heart. A man who can always lead his home toward You. A man who is not bound by fear. A man who is honest and just. A man who is not boastful or proud, except in You. A man who will protect me with his arms, his heart, his love, and his words. A man who will cherish me and will delight in finding ways to show it. A man that I could entrust my life to. A man who is in no way entangled with the world and its evils. A man . . . like You, Papa.

Many waters cannot quench love, Nor can the floods drown it. (Song of Solomon 8:7a NKJV)

12/19/04

I held a baby tonight and I was reminded of Your promise to me. Lord, sometimes my arms and my heart ache to hold a child of my own.

12/27/04

Whatever your hand finds to do, do it with your might. (Ecclesiastes 9:10a NKJV)

Lord, I always want to live this way—always about Your business. I pray that you would give me the strength to press toward the mark.

1/5/05

Lord, I cannot see Your hand, but I have to believe that You are moving. I believe that You will not leave me empty-handed.

I watched a movie that came out recently called 'National Treasure.' It's about a historian/adventurer/treasure hunter named Benjamin Franklin Gates. He has heard his whole life about a great hidden treasure. The movie takes us through scene after action-packed scene of him hunting down ancient clues.

Meanwhile, he has an enemy who tries to steal the treasure and relatives charge that he is absolutely crazy—that the treasure is a merely a myth. Still, Mr. Gates' hope will not die and he continues until the heart-pumping conclusion of the movie where he finds himself standing in the middle of an old stone cave. The treasure is missing and he is undone as he reasons, 'I just . . . really thought I was going to find the treasure.' He had thought this was it and now he is left empty-handed. Even those who called him crazy couldn't help but feel sorry for him. The waiting, searching, and working was all for nothing.

Ah! But just when you thought the final curtain was going to fall and ending credits would start rolling, the hero, Mr. Gates, gets this look on his face as if he has just had an epiphany. The music starts swelling as they find a secret door. On the other side of the door, the light from their burning torches reveals a treasure room that would make King Tut jealous. Here it is. The treasure is real. It was all worth it!

This story line deeply affected me because I, at times have felt that after waiting so long, I was standing in an empty room with promises not fulfilled and no treasure at the end of it all. In my heart, I have fought to believe that at the end of all this waiting in my personal life, God was going to do something big. There would be treasure in the end. I took such comfort in verses like this one in Isaiah:

I will give you hidden treasures, riches stored in secret places, so that you may know that I am the LORD, the God of Israel, who summons you by name. (Isaiah 45:3 NIV)

1/13/05

I stand with no one. My arms are empty of a husband and children to hold.

1/15/05

Sometimes my heart aches so much that I can feel my whole body sigh. Lord, I know You love me and You still have a plan. I feel far away from You. If this is the way that I must go, then I will go.

1/19/05

Today we went and tried on bridesmaid dresses. Lord, You already know my thoughts. You know I was wondering when it would be my turn to marry.

2/13/05

What do you think of me, Lord?

[I hear Him whisper]:

'You are my baby girl. You are so special to Me. I have kept watch over You even as a child. You allow Me to teach you. I know all that you do not. You don't have to worry or figure it out, because I know. Let My gentle breeze carry you along. You will reach the destination . . . You will.'

2/21/05

I was talking with the Lord today and I believe with all my heart that there are treasures at the end of this . . . the Promised Land.

4/7/05

Lord, I give You my future and choose not to be anxious about it anymore, knowing that You will lead me to green pastures and still waters where I will be cared for like a lamb with a loving Shepherd.

7/16/05

Oh Lord! Today we leave for Prince Edward Island. [Anne of Green Gables Land.] I am twenty-six years old and this is a dream come true for me. I feel so blessed by You. I'm going to look for You in everything.

1/31/06 Amber age 27

It is Tuesday night, Lord. You changed my life. I don't feel the same. I cried out to You and there You were. I saw a vision. It was just You and me and we were dancing. You said that You had come to take it all—all the hurt. You told me again how excited You were for the things that You have prepared for me.

2/3/06

Thank You for refining me, Lord. May I come through as pure gold.

2/4/06

'Once you are out of the wilderness, don't forget it. Remember and talk about the goodness God showed you there and how He sustained you.'

-Stormie Omartian, *Just Enough Light for the Step I'm On*[2]

2/26/06

When the LORD brought back the captivity of Zion, We were like those who dream. ²Then our mouth was filled with laughter, And our tongue with singing. Then they said among the nations, 'The LORD has done great things for them.' (Psalm 126:1-2 NKJV)

3/7/06

For You have delivered my soul from death, My eyes from tears, And my feet from falling. ⁹I will walk before the LORD in the land of the living. (Psalm 116:8-9 NKJV)

3/20/06

A man's heart plans his way, But the LORD directs his steps. (Proverbs 16:9 KJV)

Lord, I ask You to be in charge of my future. I do not want to dream dreams if You are not in them. I do not want to work hard to harvest something that will not bear fruit.

4/27/06

[In this journal entry I have written ideas about books I wanted to write and I have notes scribbled down about wanting to write a purity retreat curriculum. These projects would come to fruition many years later].

6/5/06

I surrender all of my dreams, fears, doubts, and hopes—all of them belong to You.

6/8/06

Lord, I come to You. I am Your daughter and I need the comfort of my Papa right now. I feel sad. Hide me away in the folds of Your garment. You are so kind and tender to me. You will forever be everything this heart needs.

6/13/06

[I felt the Lord say to me about my future husband]:

'Don't you know that I am molding him into My image? Did you not pray for someone like Me? Do not pine for what was when what is ahead is so much greater.'

The overwhelming ache I have felt these last weeks, Lord, it is just a glimpse of the tremendous ache You feel for me to be in Your presence. I am sorry for the many times I've caused Your heart to ache.

So the woman went her way and ate, and her face was no longer sad. (1 Samuel 1:18b NASB)

23

Harvest Is Coming

September 4, 2006 to July 16, 2009

9/4/06 Amber age 28

Lord, I feel alone and confused. I am afraid to talk to You. I have had to let my dreams die so many times that I feel paralyzed to dream anymore. I feel angry and wounded and dreadfully tired. Please come and save me. Oh, God, I know I am Your daughter and deep inside I feel like I am special to You, but my soul refuses to be comforted. I know You. You do come through. You do not fail. You are not a man that You would lie. Let Your truth penetrate every part of me. I feel like I am dying. I hurt badly and no one has words for me but You. I believe. Please help my unbelief.

Truly my soul silently waits for God; From Him comes my salvation. (Psalm 62:1 NKJV)

10/5/06

Stay with me Lord, for Your presence means more to me than my need to understand.

AMBER GALLAGHER

Now the LORD said to Samuel, 'How long will you mourn for Saul, seeing I have rejected him from reigning over Israel?' (1 Samuel 16:1a NKJV)

11/1/06

[A Friend told me today]:

'There is a time, I can see. Your children will feel blessed to have you as their mother. I can see you sitting in a chair. You will look all around and see the promise fulfilled. In that moment, you will look up to thank God. That woman afar off will know and understand what this woman does not. You'll know what all this was for and you'll be grateful for it. What you've gone through is not a punishment. It is to shape you and to give you your dreams—the ones you prayed and asked God for—the ones you told Him you wanted.'

'Sing, barren woman, you who never bore a child; burst into song, shout for joy, you who were never in labor; because more are the children of the desolate woman than of her who has a husband,' says the LORD. ²'Enlarge the place of your tent, stretch your tent curtains wide, do not hold back; lengthen your cords, strengthen your stakes. ³For you will spread out to the right and to the left; your descendants will dispossess nations and settle in their desolate cities. ⁴Do not be afraid; you will not be put to shame.' (Isaiah 54:1-3 NIV)

11/15/06

I am being made more and more aware, Lord, that You are fighting for me in ways I cannot even see. Thank you. I love You.

12/25/06

It was a really good Christmas Day. I have thought of You often. I am so blessed to have relationship with You.

11/28/07 Amber age 29

[I felt the Lord say to me]:

'Amber, I have kept my hand on you. You are My treasure. How important are your thoughts to Me. You feel a wall because there is still sadness in your heart that I had to lead you in a way you did not want to go. It was never to take away, only to position you to receive.'

1/16/08

I was telling my friend, Melissa, tonight that I just needed the Lord to shine the light on the 'treasure room.' She said, 'I can't believe you are saying this because tonight during praise and worship, I was thinking . . . Amber has followed every clue—every word from God and now she stands in the dark. She cannot see the treasure room.'

My hope soars today, Lord. Treasures out of darkness!

1/20/08

Lord, I feel You getting ready to do something. I had placed those promises on the shelf, but You have pulled them off and presented them to me once again.

3/29/08

I teach others about relationships, but I feel helpless at times in my own life.

You will show me the path of life; In Your presence is fullness of joy; At Your right hand are pleasures forevermore. (Psalm 16:11 NKJV)

AMBER GALLAGHER

6/12/08

[*The Lord made a way for me to buy a little cottage. It was truly miraculous how all the details came together. I felt as if the Lord told me that He was going to use this as an opportunity to teach me how to run a home and that I would now learn how to manage the responsibilities of it all. How exciting!*]

9/1/08 Amber age 30

Last night Melissa introduced me to a book about prayer by Becky Tirabassi. I feel like it is going to change my life.

9/5/08

Today, I praise You because You are Elohim—the Strong and Faithful One, The Only True God.

9/17/08

[*I felt the Lord say to me*]:

'I will make My will and My desires known to you. When you have no direction, stand still and see my salvation.'

It is for freedom that Christ has set us free. Stand firm, then, and do not let yourselves be burdened again by a yoke of slavery. (Galatians 5:1 NIV)

9/19/08

[*I felt the Lord say to me*]:

'I love you, Amber. It pleases Me that you come to Me with your thoughts and questions. I love that You have to know how I feel. You are sought after, My Princess. I am the only One qualified to tell you who you are and how valuable you are. No one else knows you like Me. I will never change my mind about you—ever. Go in peace.'

So that Christ may dwell in your hearts through faith. And I pray that you, being rooted and established in love, [18] may have power, together with all the saints, to grasp how wide and long and high and deep is the love of Christ, [19] and to know this love that surpasses knowledge—that you may be filled to the measure of all the fullness of God. (Ephesians 3:17-19 NIV 1984)

9/26/08

[I felt the Lord say to me]:

'I have heard your prayers and I am answering you. Your husband will treasure you. You will be My gift to him. Your home will be filled with laughter and song. The aroma of praise coming up from your home will be a sweet-smelling savor to Me. I will take great delight in you and I will dwell with you and you will know My presence.'

10/1/08

[I felt the Lord say to me]:

'When I bring you to your husband you will know peace.'

'Forget the former things; do not dwell on the past. [19] See, I am doing a new thing! Now it springs up; do you not perceive it? I am making a way in the desert and streams in the wasteland.' (Isaiah 43:18-19 NIV 1984)

10/8/08

Please bless and protect my husband. Please open up doors for him and show him Your way. Give him a wise mind and may he be passionate about me and his children. Put a song in his heart today. Make him into a priest that

AMBER GALLAGHER

I can deeply respect and fully trust so that we may walk together. Help us to be good, loving, and wise parents to the children that You entrust to us. Lord, bring us together in the beautiful way that only You can.

10/9/08

Lord, sometimes I feel like it would be easier to forget about this desire to be married—to not think about it. It feels so strong right now. I ache for him to come. I feel impassioned to pray for my husband right now. I pray that You would open up steel doors or doors that have been barred in front of him, so that he can minister before You. Preserve him. Please fill me up with You. Please bless the fruit of this womb without hesitation and without conflict or complication.

10/10/08

Lord, please rock my heart back to sleep until love needs to be awakened. I ache, Lord.

[I felt the Lord say to me]:

'It seems long and so hard, but those who sow in tears will truly reap with songs of joy. The planting has been done. It was a toilsome process, but it has been done and you have watered the seed with your tears and next—the harvest. The work will be completed. Rest now.'

10/11/08

Whether you turn to the right or to the left, your ears will hear a voice behind you, saying, 'This is the way; walk in it.' (Isaiah 30:21 NIV)

10/12/08

I pray protection today over my husband's mind. Let him be totally surrendered to You and let his ears be attuned to Your voice alone. Let him be brave. And when the time is right, let him come for me and let me know that it is him and only him. Let us support each other and always be on the same team. Let us encourage one another and sharpen each other in You and in Your Word. Oh, God if it would fit into Your plan—please bring us together soon!

[I felt the Lord say to me]:

'Amber, it will be worth the wait. You will see and know. I am the God who tears down a city and will restore it to a beautiful, glorious city. Your children will be taught by Me. I am Your God and Amber, I delight to bless you. Look around and see. You will become radiant and your heart will swell with joy because the abundance of the sea shall be turned to you. Rest, dear daughter, rest. The vision is yet for an appointed time. They will run who see it. It will be an example for all to see and glory unto My name!'

10/18/08

Lord, please protect my husband today. Bless the work of his hands. Bless his finances. Please put a guard over his mind and heart. Let him not be seduced by anyone or anything. Get us ready for the great coming together that You are planning. Let us truly leave behind the former things and perceive this new thing You are doing as it springs up.

10/21/08

Behold, the former things have come to pass, And new things I declare; Before they spring forth I tell you of them. (Isaiah 42:9 NKJV)

11/1/08

Lord, will you mention me to my husband today? I pray that his quiver would be filled and that his wife would be to him a treasure far better than rubies. Oh God, bring us to each other in Your perfect time. Help us to wait for one another and to not be weary in well doing. Oh God, let there be a time of reaping. Help us both to stay pure in word, thought, and deed before You!

[I felt the Lord say to me]:

'He is just about ready. Don't be afraid. There were some things I had to work out in order to bring about things as I had planned. He's been waiting for you too. He has asked Me the same questions as you. Oh, how good you will be together. Let your mind rest, Amber; at the appropriate time all things will be made clear. An unveiling will take place. You will be amazed and so grateful. I can already see it now. You will want this gift that I am going to offer you.'

11/3/08

Lord, I pray for my husband. I pray today You would continue to make him into a man of integrity, character, and purity. May he have such a kind, tender, and generous heart. May he be a man in love with You.

11/17/08

[I felt the Lord say to me]:

'You are single because you are chosen to walk in single-minded devotion to Me. Amber, not many will choose this path, but I tell you—it is the most rewarding. Do not waste this opportunity by wishing it away. Don't you know I could change your situation in an instant? You are doing something extra-ordinary for Me. You are finding abundant life. See this time in your life as a gift—one of the most intimate gifts that I can give you.

An unmarried woman or virgin is concerned about the Lord's affairs: Her aim is to be devoted to the Lord in both body and spirit. (1 Corinthians 7:34b NIV)

11/18/08

[I felt the Lord say to me]:

'Amber, I have a special work for you. I will instruct you. Follow My lead. I trust you with this, only be obedient to Me. Amber, I do so love you. You are Mine. I will never let you go. You are too special and you are part of Me. Let Me put My words in your mouth. Let Me use you this day. You will see. I love you.'

Later that day . . .

I know why You spoke to me this morning about being prepared. She was a young girl who thought she was pregnant and considering an abortion. We talked for an hour and You showed up for her. You stopped the world for a second to reach into her heart and let her know that she is not alone. You are with her. You saw that she was scared and overwhelmed and You wanted to set her free from fear and give her peace. I believe that You did that today. I told her about You speaking to me this morning about being ready—that You had a purpose and would give me words to speak to someone today. You said, 'Let Me use you this day. You will see.' Oh God, I see. Oh God, I am in awe—to see those tears running down her face when she realized You had sought her out today—Thank You!

11/20/08

[I felt the Lord say to me]:

'My ways are so high. They are oftentimes so confusing to the human mind, which is why trust is the key that unlocks the door to peace—so you can bear not being able to understand. I will not forsake you. The things that concern you are always before my eyes. I am aware and I will be with you. You are not alone. Be filled with hope and joy today. I am getting ready to rain down a blessing. Look for it. Perceive it. I delight to do it.'

AMBER GALLAGHER

Every word of God is pure; He is a shield to those who put their trust in Him. (Proverbs 30:5 NKJV)

11/21/08

[I felt the Lord say to me]:

'Amber, I delight to take care of you. I had to allow pain into your life. I had to allow want and need into your life in order to purify you.'

Whom have I in heaven but you? And earth has nothing I desire besides you. [26] *My flesh and my heart may fail, but God is the strength of my heart and my portion forever.* (Psalm 73:25-26 NIV)

11/29/08

I pray for my husband today. Lord, I ache for him. I want to feel his arms around me. I want to feel him touch my face. Oh God, I long to be loved deeply. Be with him today. Protect him and preserve him. I don't know what he is feeling, but I pray that You would satisfy his hunger so that he doesn't search in the arms of another woman. Let him be on fire for You. Fill him with passion and love for his God and for his wife. Bring us to each other. I believe that You are doing just that. Oh God, help me to keep walking and working. I feel like the prodigal son's father. He must have had a hard time concentrating as he would look up from the fields continually watching for the coming of his loved one.

[I felt the Lord say to me]:

'I have heard your cry. It has reached My ears and pierced My heart. That is a passionate love, Amber—to love someone so without knowing who it is—that is a gift. Amber, all will be revealed and you will know what I intend for you.'

12/6/08

[I asked the Lord]:

'Lord, where is my husband today?'

[I felt Him reply]:

'He's in the palm of My hand.'

[I said]:

'I feel so lonely for him today.'

[I felt Him reply]:

'And yet you've never been so close to him as you are today.'

Jesus replied, 'You do not realize now what I am doing, but later you will understand.' (John 13:7 NIV)

12/17/08

[I felt the Lord say to me]:

'Amber, you know My voice. Fill your mind and your heart with Me. I am leading you in the way you are to go.'

Delight yourself in the LORD and he will give you the desires of your heart. (Psalm 37:4 NIV)

12/26/08

Lord, I come to You as Ruth asking you to send me a kinsmen redeemer. I come to You as Mary asking for a miracle and a life of destiny. I come to

AMBER GALLAGHER

You as Hannah asking You to fill this womb with babies. I come to You as Mary sitting at Your feet realizing only You can satisfy this hungry heart. I know You are putting all the pieces together. I will wait for You. Please quiet my heart. Please cover my husband tonight. Let him present his loneliness to You as an offering of praise. Bring him through and give him complete peace in this journey. Purify us. Make us ready to be one. Help us. We are desperate for Your covering right now.

12/27/08

In him our hearts rejoice, for we trust in his holy name. (Psalm 33:21 NIV)

1/16/09

It is supposed to be below zero degrees today. Dr. Brickner [my chiropractor] asked mom if I'd be interested in meeting his brother-in-law, Brian Gallagher. He said that he was a good Christian guy and that he was nice looking. Lord, should I say yes? God, please guide me in this. I don't know what I'm doing.

(Pete Esposito also called me at work today and told me about Brian Gallagher.)

1/17/09

May God himself, the God of peace, sanctify you through and through. May your whole spirit, soul and body be kept blameless at the coming of our Lord Jesus Christ. [24]*The one who calls you is faithful and he will do it.* (1 Thessalonians 5:23-24 NIV 1984)

1/19/09

A friend prayed over me yesterday that it would be very soon . . . that there was a divine appointment just ahead and that these feet could not afford to go in the wrong direction.

1/20/09

I got an e-mail from Brian Gallagher. He seems really nice. He asked me if we could go to dinner sometime soon.

[I hear]:

'Do not be afraid.'

1/21/09

[I felt the Lord say to me]:

'You will be so blessed by My gifts to you. Oh, I am excited. Wait in expectation. I will do much for you and on your behalf.'

2/4/09

Bless my husband today—deliver him from every attempt of the enemy for his life. Heal him, free him, and guide him in all truth.

3/28/09

[I felt the Lord say to me]:

Amber, I have not forgotten you nor have I forgotten My promises concerning you. Rise up and be blessed, child. Watch for My promises to be fulfilled concerning your life.

3/29/09

There is a part of me that really wants to lay some busyness aside in order to focus on speaking, writing, and developing a balanced life.

AMBER GALLAGHER

5/18/09

He gives the childless woman a family, making her a happy mother. Praise the Lord. Praise the Lord! (Psalm 113:9 NLT)

[I attended a ladies' encounter this past weekend. I had such breakthrough and heaviness began to lift off me. I was once and for all released from an emotionally draining relationship that had lingered off and on for years. God used one testimony, in particular, to really speak to me about walking in the deliverance that was already given to me by God. Something truly changed that day for good.]

6/17/09

I went and talked to mom and dad about the feelings I have been having for some time about leaving my church. Dad prayed over me this really beautiful prayer for Your will. He said tonight that he felt I was spent and needed to be free to pursue the dreams that the Lord has placed on my heart. I felt relief. It is sad, but somehow it is right.

6/18/09

Thank you for hearing dad's prayer yesterday. He prayed exactly what was in my heart.

[I felt the Lord say to me]:

'Amber, I know that you would follow Me to the ends of the earth. I am showing you the way and I will protect you.'

6/20/09

I did an awesome video study this morning of Beth Moore's book, 'Esther: It's Tough Being a Woman.' God, I really feel that You are leading me. Mrs. Moore talked about 'The Human Dilemma of Destiny.'

'We can be one decision away from breaking the old story line and beginning a new chapter of the narrative . . . one decision away from the most important turn in your entire path.'

-Beth Moore, *Esther: It's Tough Being a Woman*[1]

I told [my friend] Emma that I was leaving. She told me that when I told her this, she saw a mental picture of a bird being released from a cage and spreading its wings to fly free.

[This was pretty amazing since I have viewed myself like a bird trapped in a cage wanting to be free.]

Lord, let it be unto me as You have said. I will go.

6/21/09

It's Father's Day. Wherever my husband is today, please fill up his loneliness and give him hope today as he waits for his quiver to be full.

6/23/09

Tonight is my last youth service. Wow, Lord, help me to do all of this correctly. Help them to know that I love them. Lord, you healed me on that stage singing with the praise team over and over again. I thank you for the honor of serving You and serving all of those young people for nine years. It was hard and it was great. Thank You.

Lord, bless my husband. May Your work be accomplished through him today. Lord, let him know that I'm coming!

7/3/09

I don't know which way to turn,
You say life abundant, but I still fill the loss behind me.

AMBER GALLAGHER

You have called me out to walk alone.
You say You will guide, and I can hear Your voice behind me.

I come running to Your arms,
You say You will catch me and I can feel Your arms around me.

7/14/09

Lord, I can feel you nudging my heart—'The Princess Within' program will become a purity curriculum that can be made available to churches and for conferences. Lord, is that from You? I can see it. Oh God, this is exciting!

7/15/09

I woke up this morning excited about the possibilities of 'The Princess Within.' Lord, I feel like You are really going to do something with this. Oh, please help me. Pour Yourself through me and show me the way. In Jesus' Name.

[I felt the Lord say to me]:

'Didn't I tell you to watch and see what I would do? I desire to bless you and take care of you. This is no hard thing for Me. Watch for My hand and you will see it. I am doing a great work before you.'

7/16/09

[I felt the Lord say to me]:

'I will open up doors before you and you will proclaim My truth. Be bold and be ready.'

24

Songs of Joy

August 2, 2009 to October 5, 2010

8/2/09 Amber age 31

Everywhere I turn, I keep hearing about the journey . . . leaving the old behind and stepping out into destiny.

9/25/09

'It's marvelous to be known by God. How thankful I am that I have no need to explain to Him every smirk or wince or chuckle or tear as they each come into my life. He knows it all completely.'

-Michael Warden, Alone with God[1]

9/27/09

[I felt the Lord say to me]:

'I know that you are not exactly sure where we are going, but you are trusting Me and that gives Me joy, daughter. It is time to be free and soar

AMBER GALLAGHER

with wings like eagles—to run and not be weary. I am about to open the doors. Run!'

This is what the LORD says—your Redeemer, the Holy One of Israel: 'I am the LORD your God, who teaches you what is best for you, who directs you in the way you should go.' (Isaiah 48:17 NIV)

9/29/09

Lord, wherever my husband is today, I pray that he would feel the warmth of your presence. Flood his soul and fill his car right at this moment, I pray.

10/12/09

Lord, do you want to me write a retreat curriculum for boys? Please give me ideas.

10/15/09

I feel like this is how I will feel about my marriage and family:

So that people may see and know, may consider and understand, that the hand of the LORD has done this, that the Holy One of Israel has created it. (Isaiah 41:20 NIV)

This also reminds me of what Elizabeth said after she found out that she was pregnant after waiting for such a long time:

'The Lord has done this for me,' she said. 'In these days he has shown his favor and taken away my disgrace among the people.' (Luke 1:25 NIV 1984)

[I did not feel disgraced about being single, but I did feel that a few people got tired of watching and waiting with me. I never wanted my story to be a discouragement to those who were waiting to see what God would do. I gave those feelings to the Lord. He is able to handle His own reputation.

I did look at these words spoken by Elizabeth as hopeful for my own circumstances. I knew that my 'one day' would come too.]

10/16/09

[I felt the Lord say to me]:

'You are not forgotten. If you could but see what is just ahead of you. Take heart. Trust Me!'

'The enemy will tell you that while God is taking care of everyone else—including all of your friends who are getting married—He has somehow forgotten about you. It's a lie!'

-Janet Folger, *What's a Girl to Do While Waiting for Mr. Right?*[2]

11/11/09

I once heard a quote by Amy Carmichael, a missionary to India that went: 'It is a safe thing to trust Him to fulfill the desire which He creates.' How true!

Let us hold tightly without wavering to the hope we affirm, for God can be trusted to keep his promise. [24]*Let us think of ways to motivate one another to acts of love and good works.* (Hebrews 10:23-24 NLT)

11/16/09

Lord, I know that Your eyes are on me and Your hands are guiding me. You have not forgotten. Bless You!

11/25/09

Lord, You are what I am grateful for most of all. I love Your presence.

AMBER GALLAGHER

[I felt the Lord say to me]:

'*Amber, I am doing a work. Watch it unfold before you. See this new thing; perceive it as it springs up before you. I will raise you to lead an army. Their hearts will be won in My name. I have given you the keys. Honor Me! I will go before you, preparing the way—I will whisper in the gatekeeper's ear and doors will be opened before you! Keep your eyes ever on Me and I will show you the way. You will freely walk through the doors. Do not be afraid. Be bold and proclaim My words from the rooftop. I will be there.*'

12/1/09

I have been going to counseling. [Many of my journal entries during this time were about the lies I had previously believed and am now replacing with God's truth.]

12/2/09

[I felt the Lord say to me]:

'*Peace, be still. I have promised to take care of you and I am committed to that promise. I will hold you together and I will put the pieces into place. Do not waver! Daughter, I see your need and I am here.*'

12/17/09

I was sitting here thinking about it . . . this time last year as we began to start a new year. I remember that I was pretty apprehensive. Everyone in our ladies Bible study was telling about the new things that they felt stirring in their lives. I was silent because I didn't have a clue. As I look back, this year has become one the most hopeful and exciting years of my life. I have written 'The Princess Within' and 'The Sacred Revolution' Bible study curricula and it turns out that I have had several opportunities to sing and speak. I am excited to get to do something I dearly love to do.

Lord, wherever my husband is tonight, please give him strength, peace, guidance, and deliverance. I pray that his heart would truly hunger for Your word.

12/18/09

Lord, I pray over 'The Princess Within.' I pray over these future events and the girls who will attend. Let them be set free and set on fire to take their God-given roles as daughters of the King. Let them truly walk in victory and power. Let them be overcomers as they trample over their enemies.

12/19/09

Lord, please secure my husband. Fill him with a renewed mind and heart. Let him walk in great victory today. I pray for a turnaround in his life. Pull him up close to You. May he look, talk, and love like You. Open up the doors that he has been praying for.

1/1/10

Happy New Year! Last night, Carla and I got together and ate appetizers. Then, we went over to Tracy Esposito's house. We ate pizza and got her sons to pull out their keyboard and guitar. We sang for about an hour. It was really fun. We laughed so much. Thank you, Lord, for a great start to a great year.

Since Tracy happens to be Brian's sister, guess who was also there? Yep, Brian joined in on the guitar playing and singing. We all stayed and talked until three in the morning.

1/6/10

Lord, I pray for my husband. Be with him. Give him strength and help him to be courageous.

AMBER GALLAGHER

1/8/10

I am consumed today with the prayer, 'Lord, You don't forget.'

1/10/10

[I felt the Lord say to me]:

'Daughter, the message this morning was about metamorphosis. That is where you are. You will be a brand new daughter at the end of this. No longer will you minister out of pain and sorrow, but you will minister out of joy and victory. You will see a difference. It will be evident to all. I love you, little dove, be free!'

For you shall go out with joy, And be led out with peace; The mountains and the hills shall break forth into singing before you, And all the trees of the field shall clap their hands. (Isaiah 55:12 NKJV)

1/19/10

Brian was working at the center again . . .

1/28/10

God, Brian?

2/1/10

[I felt the Lord say to me]:

Relax and trust in Me. Amber, I guard over your way. Look back and see the times where I have kept you from catastrophe. I have kept you, daughter

2/3/10

[A Prayer for Brian Gallagher]:

Direct us both, Papa. Give each of us boldness and courage. Help us to be friends and if You want more than that please make it clear to us. Protect us both and help us to be in Your will.

[I felt the Lord say to me]:

'Take a breath. Let me lead and we will dance through this together—every step, around every corner, we will take it together. Bless you, daughter.'

2/7/10

Tonight, I am going with Carla to Pete and Tracy Esposito's house. Brian will be there. Lord, I have no idea what I am doing. Please lead and guide me as You promised.

2/14/10

Today has been a really great day. Happy Valentine's Day, Jesus! I love You so much.

2/16/10

God, it is obvious that You are the best at knowing who I need for a husband. Guide me and let me not settle for my own will. Bring him soon. Help me to know when he is here.

2/17/10

Brain was at the center fixing something again today . . .

AMBER GALLAGHER

2/20/10

I am to meet Brian and the whole family for bowling. We are getting something to eat and then coming back to mom and dad's house for a game night.

Lord, please forgive me. So many times I find myself getting anxious in the waiting. I am sorry. You never leave anything unfinished.

The boundary lines have fallen for me in pleasant places; indeed, I have a beautiful inheritance. (Psalm 16:6 HCSB)

2/21/10

It has been an overwhelming day. My car got stuck in the snow again and I almost took out the neighbor's fence. My gutter fell, tearing off siding and breaking down my fence. I sent a message for all my girls to pray. I am feeling better already. Thank You for always providing the funds and resources to keep moving. I'm sorry that I wanted to scream, 'Why aren't You taking care of me?' I know You are.

2/28/10

Lord, I don't want to be alone anymore. Last night at the family game night, it was awesome to be surrounded by a huge family that loves You and loves each other. I am asking and I know that You will lead me in the way that I should go. I do want to be a wife and mother. Show me Your way that I may walk with You.

3/3/10

You will keep him in perfect peace, Whose mind is stayed on You, Because he trusts in You. (Isaiah 26:3 NKJV)

3/5/10

Brian and I are going out by ourselves to dinner tomorrow. I am still chewing on the messages I got from my devotion this morning: How many times did the Lord tell His people, 'Do not be afraid?'

'You will have a river of fear standing between you and your promised land, but you will have to cross it scared if need be. The thing that you are scared of is probably the thing you are supposed to do. Your promised land is not something you can do in your own strength.'

-Beth Moore, Esther: It's Tough Being a Woman[3]

3/13/10

I came home, exercised, and cleaned my house—a very 'unromantic' way to spend a Friday evening and I enjoyed it.

3/14/10

Lord, I pray that You would give Brian direction. Help me to be an encouraging friend.

3/20/10

Tonight, we are having another game night. Everyone is coming. Brian is coming over to fix my roof, gutter, and fence. Thank you, Lord, for taking care of these things. I am grateful.

3/24/10

After work, I met Brian. We went to the driving range and hit some golf balls. Then, we went and ate at Longhorn. It was really fun.

AMBER GALLAGHER

3/25/10

Lord, please guide our friendship and make Your will clearly known.

3/3/10

Lord, wherever my husband is today, please bless him with goodness, favor, and unspeakable joy. Let him be filled with Your wonder. Bless him, Papa.

4/4/10

I went to brunch at Melissa Brickner's after church. I feel like I am becoming a better person by being around this family. I feel like the season of my life is getting ready to change again.

4/6/10

Brian called me around 9:30 p.m. We talked until 12:30 a.m. Lord, please direct me. He is such a good man and I really like being around him.

4/12/10

Yesterday, I went to church. Afterward, Brian came and picked me up. He stepped out of the car with this beautiful bouquet of flowers. We went to a steakhouse and then got some frozen custard.

4/25/10

Lord, I am falling for Mr. Brian Gallagher. Last night in the car, Lexy, my niece, said, 'I can't wait until you get married cause I want to have a little brother or sister.' Too cute! [I have to assume she meant 'little cousin' instead.]

Also, last night while we were sitting at the dinner table, we were all holding hands for prayer. Brian's little nephew, Gideon, said, 'Uncle Bird, it would be good if you married Amber.'

I said, 'Really?'

Brian said, 'Thank you!'

Everyone laughed. Little Gideon was like, 'What did I say?' with his innocent facial expression.

Brian called me on the way home. We talked about our experiences with the Lord and what we felt it meant for wives and husbands to submit to one another.

4/26/10

I woke up this morning feeling light in my heart. Thank You, God. I keep thinking of the verse in Proverbs 13:12 (NKJV) 'Hope deferred makes the heart sick, But when the desire comes, it is a tree of life.'

4/28/10

Last night, after Bible study, I went to Tracy's for little Rachel's birthday party. Brian put together my garden greenhouse. It was so sweet. Lord, am I falling in love with this man? Oh God, please help me to choose wisely. Please, make your will perfectly clear to both Brian and me. Lord, I love being around this family where some little person is always having a birthday and the house is always filled.

5/3/10

Last night's service was awesome. Thank You! Brian called and we talked until about 12:30 a.m. Lord, thank you for giving me a friend in Brian. He seems to be a man after Your heart. He is teachable.

AMBER GALLAGHER

[I felt the Lord say to me]:

'You are beginning to feel the droplets that are preceding an abundance of rain. You will see what it is like for those who love their God. I will display My glory through your marriage. I will show Myself strong and mighty on your behalf. Watch and see if I will not do this. I am with you, daughter. Stand and be amazed.'

5/5/10

I was struck by the verse that says, You led the children of Israel to a land that you had 'searched out for them' (Ezekiel 20:6). I believe this is true about the husband You will give me. You have searched out a husband for me and I believe that he will be Your man for me. Thank You that this is not a choice I have to make on my own.

5/7/10

Last night, Brian and I had a really deep conversation about boundaries. God, he has been so respectful. Please guide us both. God, his prayer last night was precious. I can't help but feel that it was special to You, too. Please give us grace. Lord, I think that I love Brian! Please guard my heart and mind with Your peace.

5/8/10

Oh God, this weekend has been so beautiful. We all went bowling. Brian held my hand. It was so sweet.

5/9/10

It's Mother's Day and I was just writing in my 'future husband' journal [a gift that I will give him one day] about how I dream of being a mother and then this message came from Brian:

'Hey, good morning and happy mother's day! I know you are not a mom quite yet, but to the One who sees eternity you are, and for that we will celebrate you today!'

Brian did celebrate me as being a mother all day. He picked me up and we went and hit golf balls with my new pink golf bag and clubs he got me. He says that I am really good, which I find surprising. Then, we went to the Macaroni Grill. Before we went into the restaurant, Brian took my hand and said, 'Amber, I love you and I don't know if it's too soon to tell you.' He said he had felt that way for a long time. I was thrilled! Oh God, I do love him too.

5/11/10

Last night, Brian and I got to talk about a lot of things. I definitely like how he handles conflict. I told him last night that I loved him. Oh God, I ask for Your protection and Your grace.

5/12/10

I asked Brian how long he had felt like he loved me. He said he thought it was when I went away for the ladies' Women of Joy weekend conference back in April. I think I started feeling something when I found out that he had worked through 'The Princess Within.' Then, of course, during our conversation that Sunday night when I returned from Women of Joy, I saw the Holy Spirit move and bring us onto the same page.

Brian told me that his mom would have loved me and then he said, 'It makes me sad a little.' He went on to tell me that I was one of a kind ... that I am all he has ever wanted and more. Then he said, 'I feel like I'm on the verge of TMI (Too Much Information).' He stopped himself.

Lord, if he wants to marry me ...

AMBER GALLAGHER

5/16/10

We babysat the Brickner kids. Watching Brian interact with those kids was one of the most beautiful things that I have ever seen. Lord, I would love to spend the rest of my life with him. Lord, I have never felt like this. I need Your guidance.

[I felt the Lord say to me]:

'Amber, I am so thrilled about the plans that I have for you. I will help you and be your Strength. I will show you the way of life, truth, purity, and goodness.'

5/17/10

Brian and I had a really great conversation last night. We want to marry each other. We are fasting and praying for the next three Tuesdays. We are believing that You are going to teach us the way that we should go. We are just two people trying to know and love You with these lives. Oh God, let us see and marvel at the works of Your hands—the things You do on behalf of those who love You.

God, You have spoken to me time and again about how excited You are. You are the Master Storyteller—all Your ways are lovely. You make all things beautiful in Your time.

5/24/10

I am watching You literally give this little bird beside my car an abundance of food and I am reminded of the scripture that talks about how You take care of the birds and notice when one of them falls to the ground. How much more care You take in showing us Your love and provision!

5/25/10

Last night, Brian told me that he knows it's me. He said that he felt like his search was over. Lord, May all who look on and see what You have done, declare Your name to be the name above every name. Nothing is impossible for You.

5/26/10

[I felt the Lord say to me]:

'Amber, I love you, dear little girl. I am moving on your behalf in ways that you cannot see or even understand. Keep surrendering your way to Me and I will keep showing you the path that leads to eternal life.'

5/27/10

[After asking Him to make provision for Brian and me to get married, I felt the Lord say]:

'I will cover you with My feathers and under My wings shall you take refuge. Take heart. I am making a way.'

He will cover you with his feathers. He will shelter you with his wings. His faithful promises are your armor and protection. (Psalm 91:4 NLT)

Thank You, Lord!

5/28/10

Lord, I am blown away by Your goodness. I love You! I love You! I love You! I feel like Brian is going to be my husband.

AMBER GALLAGHER

6/1/10

Last night, we went to Tracy's where we played wiffle ball and had a bonfire. As we were saying goodbye out by the car, Brian said, 'Someday, it will be different.' He said this because we didn't want to say goodbye.

'When is some day?' I asked.

'In the fall?' he questioned.

Oh Lord, is that Your will for us? I do want to marry him. I have never really felt completely comfortable with anyone. Always before, talking about 'future things' with other guys would give me an uneasy feeling, but Lord, with Brian, I feel completely comfortable with it. I am trusting that You are showing two young people, madly in love with You, the way to Your heart.

6/2/10

I am starting to gear up for 'The Princess Within' summer camps. Lord, I ask for Your guidance, blessing, and provision.

6/26/10

Brian went to mom and dad's while I was gone to the Home School Convention. He talked with my parents and grandparents for about an hour around the dinner table. Then, Brian asked to talk to dad. He told him that we want to marry each other and asked if dad had any objections to this. Dad told him that they were in support of us one hundred percent and they felt like Brian was going to be really good for me.

6/28/10

I have returned from the convention. Yesterday, Brian and I went to church and then down to the Newport on the levy. We watched the Red's *game, got Italian ice, and saw a movie. Afterwards, we went to eat and walked on the Purple People Bridge. We sat on one of the benches and talked about where we would want to go on our honeymoon. It was beautiful. The cityscape was awesome. Brian kissed me on the cheek and prayed over us. He thanked God for me and said that I was like home to him. It was such a beautiful day.*

7/3/10

God, You thought of everything. I could feel that You were with us. I feel Your blessing. My heart is grateful that You know what we need and that You never forget. You will bring to pass all that You have spoken. I am so in love with You. My heart sings Your praise today. You have turned my sadness into joy.

10/5/10 Amber age 32

This time in my life is completely unexpected. I never would have imagined what You would give me and I am grateful for Your plan, Lord. Oh, to see how You have opened all of these doors in my life and allowed Brian in—I feel like You have given my heart to him. I was thinking again today how last year I had asked You if my husband could enter into my life by the end of the year and on New Year's Eve, Brian walked in for good.

This is a new chapter. My life will never be the same . . .

When Dreams Come True

25

You've Got Mail!

"Pete Esposito's on the line for you," my friend and co-worker, Tracey, called to me from her office.

Pete owned the local mechanic shop as well as a T-shirt business. I assumed that he must be calling about the latest T-shirt project we had going for the Pregnancy Center since my car hadn't been in the shop recently.

"Ok, thanks!" I replied, wondering why he didn't talk to Tracey about those T-shirts.

When I said hello, Pete began to tell me about an altogether different reason for his call. He asked if I would be interested in meeting his brother-in-law, Brian Gallagher. I was pretty hesitant about these types of conversations. I wondered if Pete knew that my chiropractor, Dr. Brickner, had already mentioned this same guy, Brian, to me. Both of these men were each married to one of Brian's sisters. (I was surrounded!) I politely listened to all of the adjectives and accomplishments he used to describe this fine, Christian man. As Pete continued, I felt a small twinge of hope start to build. It was certainly intriguing.

Most "opportunities" in my life had turned out to be either seriously wrong or relationships in which I lacked a certain amount of peace, yet I felt hopeful with a measure of readiness in my heart. At the same time, I was careful to move cautiously so as not to get carried away. Pete asked if he could give Brian my number, but I preferred to start by e-mailing and with that, a few days later, I received my first e-mail introduction from a Mr. Brian Gallagher:

Sunday, January 18, 2009

Amber,

Hi there. My name is Brian Gallagher. Pete Esposito (my brother-in-law) gave me your e-mail address and said that it would be okay for me to take a moment to contact you. He shared with me a little bit about your background and life focus... which is impressive. Pete speaks very highly of you, which tells me that you have a genuine nature and are a woman of faith.

He also shared with me that you work with the Community Pregnancy Center and are also involved with your church community. It must be very rewarding to be a source of light and encouragement to young people in a desperate and life-changing situation! How long have you been with CPC? I understand that you are a gifted singer/musician as well. My musical abilities are fractional at best, but that doesn't stop me. Do you also play a musical instrument?

Well, there are a lot of other things that I would like to learn and share with you, but for the sake of time and space initially, I just thought that I would send you a quick e-mail to say hello and introduce myself. Maybe we can get together to fill in some of the gaps at some point?

Have a great day and I look forward to hearing from you.

Brian

Monday, January 19, 2009

Hey Brian Gallagher,

Thank you for your kind words. Pete speaks very highly of you too . . . and so does Dr. B.

Let's see, to answer your questions . . . Yes, I work at the CPC doing the Abstinence Program in schools and youth groups and such. I love it and I've been here for a little over seven years now. It's always an adventure working in this field with teenagers.

What do you do for a living?

And yes, I do love to sing. Someone asked me this weekend how long I've been singing. I believe since birth. Growing up, my dad was a minister of youth and music, so naturally, my brother and I were always singing. We practically lived at church and were involved in just about everything. I play keyboard, not as well as I'd like to, but I love it. This weekend I played for a ladies retreat. It was a lot of fun.

Do you play an instrument or sing?

Brian, would you mind telling me about your relationship with the Lord? Sure, I can hang out sometime if you'd like.

Thank you for writing, Brian. Have a wonderful day!

Amber

AMBER GALLAGHER

Monday, January 19, 2009

Amber,

Thank you for your e-mail and candid inquiry about my relationship with Jesus. It is refreshing to come across a woman who is immediately open to my faith.

There are many ways (and stories) that I could share in an effort to try and communicate the fullness of my relationship with Jesus, but to put it into a word I would have to say that my relationship with Him is dynamic. This may seem basic but for me it has been a revelation over time, because I have found that after many years of walking with God, that my ways are clearly not His ways, but He has been so patient and faithful to me. I am forever changed and being changed. Does that make sense? Honestly, sometimes it's been really hard, but in the end there is always repentance, forgiveness, and a deeper knowledge of His goodness. I would be happy to share more later.

How about you, how would you describe your relationship?

Regarding my job, I design/develop sports equipment.

Relative to my musical abilities . . . I read a few years ago that the rocks will cry out if we cease to praise. That stuck with me and over time I decided that I was smarter and more valuable than a stone, so I bought a guitar and started to learn how to play a couple chords. I'm still not very good, but to this day I have not yet heard a stone sing. So, I must be doing something right?

Maybe I can meet you for dinner upcoming if you have time?

Brian

Tuesday, January 20, 2009

Hey Brian,

Dynamic . . . that makes a lot of sense. I have found that learning the 'His ways are not mine' lesson is a pretty hard lesson to learn.

Well, I would call my story with Christ, 'The Great Love Affair.' (I am what I call a hopeful romantic.) He has become my Everything and I find that I am complete because of Him. I get up everyday and cannot wait to hear what He has to say to me. I have loved the Lord my whole life, but I will say the story gets really good around age 20 . . . oh, then 23. I continue to be amazed.

Pete was telling me about some sort of bat you invented? Nice.

I'd say if the stones aren't singing, you're doing good! I think that you picking up the guitar is really great. We never get good at anything until we first start, right?

Sure, I like to eat. When did you have in mind?

Amber

I thought perhaps you'd like to read portions of our story through Brian's perspective. It may help you to consider that your future husband is waiting for you as you are for him. God is doing a work on both ends of the spectrum. You are certainly not alone in this.

A Word from Brian . . .

The first time I met Amber was for dinner and I have to admit that my expectations were fairly low as my senses were frayed from years of dating well-intended women who were visions of loveliness, but lacked authentic spiritual backbone. As a single man who spent several years alone, allowing God to do his work in me, I removed myself from the cares of 'dating life' until I could gain a clearer perspective about life and love and how to find both.

As time passed, I slowly emerged with a better understanding of God's way in searching for a life companion and not coincidentally, I found that purity was at the centerpiece of His way. Fast forward a year later and I was given the opportunity to meet Amber for the first time.

26

The Lady in the Red Coat

Brian Gallagher walked through the door of my favorite restaurant on January 24, 2009. I told him that he could watch for the lady in the red coat.

I had arrived a little early and sat nervously waiting. My mind was reeling, *What would he be like in person? Would the conversation flow or would it be awkward? Oh, I hope it's not going to be awkward.*

Brian arrived and we were immediately shown to our seats. We ended up talking for hours about our life experiences as well as our relationships with God. One thing I always remembered clearly was how kind and respectful Brian seemed. He opened my car door, which was an indication of old-school manners. That is a trait I found quite impressive.

A Word from Brian . . .

After years of successfully wading through a sea of pretenders, disappointment gave root to a lie, which ultimately led to failure. I heard once that a counterfeit usually comes before the prize and I certainly found that to be true. After a couple years of soul searching, God's mercy brought me to a spacious place and a new resolve to protect myself from the traps of dating.

AMBER GALLAGHER

It's amazing how God works. For years Amber was a family friend hiding in plain sight and while I knew of her, we had never officially met. Before my mom passed away, she and my sisters became involved with Amber's pregnancy center and that was the start of what ultimately turned out to be a series of divine appointments, oddly enough orchestrated by my sisters' husbands. While I knew of Amber, I still had some reluctance in light of my past experience.

I finally came to the proper conclusion that God would not cast me off forever, so after a couple of introductory e-mails back and forth, we decided to meet for dinner. I was told that she would be the one in the 'red coat.'

As I said before, I was cautious, but silently optimistic. I remember walking through the door of the restaurant and quickly scanning the room for a red coat, but nothing stood out. I briefly checked in with the receptionist and as I turned, I saw a beautiful woman with a red coat sitting down, quietly talking on the phone.

In a moment, I turned from a confident eligible suitor, into a nervous wreck. Fortunately for me, by the time she stood up to greet me, the Holy Spirit kicked in and she was none the wiser. In my mind I couldn't believe how beautiful she was—and she was a Christian!

Keep in mind that my experiences in dating thus far had proven that beautiful women somehow think that they are exempt from God's way so I was delighted to learn over the course of a two-hour dinner that she made no claim of exemption . . . quite the opposite. It was the best experience that I have ever had. The conversation was easy, light hearted, but also had reasonable depth.

After dinner, I was happy to call it a night and quit while I was ahead, but Amber asked if I wanted to go to next door to Graeter's for ice cream and I jumped at the opportunity. We spent another hour-and-a-half talking about things of greater importance and during that time, it felt like we were both soaking it in. I could tell by then that she was an uncommon woman and I definitely wanted to learn more about her.

At the end of the night, I confidently walked Amber to her car, thanked her for her time, and quietly started looking forward to seeing her again.

* * * *

The next morning was Sunday. I read a devotional during my quiet time that gave me pause. The author told a particular story about a man and woman who cared about each other, but untimely circumstances prohibited them from being together. It spoke of the woman giving this relationship opportunity one more chance.

It was uncanny how the details of this story described a former relationship that I thought was long over. I wrestled with questions this devotional stirred in my heart for several hours. I wondered if God was leading me to give this previous attachment one last opportunity for a turnaround. Conflicted, yet feeling urged, I went to this man and told him what I had read. After a long conversation, we decided to try and make things work.

I knew that I would have to let Brian know about this latest development. I sent one final e-mail:

I wanted to thank you again for the lovely dinner and the ice cream. It was really nice. In the small amount of time I've known you, you seem like a really great man of God. I wanted to let you know about something . . .

Without going into lots of detail, in a turn of events, I had a conversation last evening with a man for whom I have previously had feelings. It was something that I thought was finished long ago, but it was reopened and it turns out that I need to take the time to see what this conversation has brought up. So, I feel that to be respectful to you and of my need to see some things through, unfortunately, I will not be able to go out with you again.

I pray the very best for you. I know a woman of God will cherish the godly Christian man that you are. And again, I'm sorry. I really did not expect it all to come about as it has. I hope that you understand.

Thank you, Brian.

AMBER GALLAGHER

A Word from Brian . . .

After dinner, on the following evening, I received an e-mail from Amber explaining that she had a great time, but that she needed to take time to work through some things in her life. I immediately called my sister, Tracy, and told her about the e-mail, all the while hiding my profound disappointment. I remember sitting in my car after I hung up with Tracy, trying to keep an 'oh well' attitude with God, rationalizing that He must have someone else better for me. Inwardly, it hurt. I had never met a woman with such virtue.

27

"I Still Love You!"

It only took a few short weeks to see that there was not going to be a future possibility with this former romantic interest. I wondered why I would feel urged to go back to this relationship when it was only going to end in more heartache and disappointment. I have come to believe that God orchestrated a "last try" so that I could finally have closure on a long, drawn-out ordeal.

I ended things with this guy for what would be the last time. I was a little surprised at the lack of sadness I felt over it. Instead, I felt a huge burden lifted and a surge of relief had taken its place. I had no more questions. I had my answer to "What if?"

I began to voraciously throw myself into reading the Bible and prayer time with God. I went through a life-changing study on the book of Esther. I read how Esther moved out of her comfort zone as she walked through the doors of destiny that landed her in the palace positioned to save her people from certain enemies who threatened to annihilate them. I can't say my situation was quite as dramatic, but I can say that I felt my doors of destiny were swinging open as the Lord began to stir my heart. I felt Him drawing me away from not only my current positions of leadership, but away from the church that I had attended for the past twelve years.

I had actively volunteered, immersing myself in church work for as long as I could remember. In fact, the last couple of years of what felt like a full-time church work career I completed in a constant state of exhaustion and burnout. However, this was life as I had known it and yet here I was sensing that the Lord wanted to move me. I eventually heard these words in my spirit, "Come away." I struggled with what that meant. I had so many questions. In response, I would hear the Lord again, "Come away." During an intense devotional time while taking Beth Moore's Esther study, I read about how it did not make sense and the timing didn't seem right for Esther to move. However, she picked up and left life as she knew it.[1] I had to obey or be miserable. So, I did it. I resigned from my positions having no idea where I was going to eventually end up.

Sacred Revolution Ministries

My last youth service marked the end of almost a decade of being the worship leader for our church's youth department. The Lord had nudged my heart with the idea to start Sacred Revolution Ministries about a year back—a ministry on a mission to *inspire and equip people for the sacred life with Christ*. The moment I got home from this last service, the Lord opened up Heaven and like raindrops, ideas started pouring into my mind. I would write purity curricula for girls and one for guys too. In about ten months I had my first Bible study published, *The Princess Within: Living Like a Princess from the Inside Out*. In the following year, a second Bible study, *The Sacred Revolution: Uncovering Purity for the Modern-Day Knight* would be printed. At present, we have been privileged to conduct numerous Bible study classes, camps, and weekend retreats.

A Bird in a Cage

After leaving all that was familiar, I ended up attending a church called Calvary. I would come in and cry—a lot. This was partly because I felt homesick and partly because the Lord was opening up doors in my heart which let the hurt spill out of me like a rushing river current.

On Sunday mornings during the praise and worship time, the young people would do what they called "worship art." While the songs would fill the sanctuary, someone would paint a particular God-inspired design. One such morning, a couple of young ladies painted this beautiful picture of a birdcage. On the outside of this empty cage was a bird in the hand of Jesus with a caption that read, "Do not be bound, but rest in the peace and freedom of the Father's hand." When the picture became clear, my mouth dropped open and I began to cry. The memory of a conversation I had years ago came to mind. In exasperation, I lamented to a dear mentor of mine that I felt like a bird caught in a cage. I had survived a couple of broken relationships that left me mentally and emotionally exhausted with a load of baggage that weighed heavily on my heart and mind. I felt trapped in my circumstances. Yet, in this glorious instant, at Calvary, I knew with increasing certainty that with every stroke of these ladies' brushes, the last inches of my cage door were being peeled back by the strong, unseen hand of my Savior. Of course, there were several experiences and encounters leading up to this liberating moment, but I was finally free and Jesus had me exactly where I was supposed to be—on my knees at Calvary, freely resting in the palm of His hand. When I see an empty birdcage, my heart leaps a little. It is not merely a beautiful piece of home décor, but instead, it has become a symbol of freedom.

Transition to Position

During all this time, I wondered aloud to a couple of close friends, "I can't help but think that God may be healing me and positioning me to be a wife and mother." I always used to wonder with my extremely busy life how I would possibly have time to cultivate a relationship with a prospective husband, much less get married and start a family. I knew something would have to change.

Numerous times I would praise the Lord for these single years and yet I would find myself praying, "Lord, I know that You won't forget about me, but please . . . don't forget." It was one of those, "I believe, please help my unbelief" dilemmas. He would always remind me that He had big plans and was really excited to reveal them to me when the time was right.

During my big "Esther move" and the consequent healing I was receiving, I made a bold request, "Lord, You surely don't have to do this, but would You bring my future husband into my life by the end of this year? Regardless, I still love You!" I did not know that the Lord had intentionally transitioned me in order to position me for a new chapter where I would see prayers answered and promises fulfilled.

The Community Pregnancy Center

It was our 2009 annual fundraising banquet for the Community Pregnancy Center where I had worked for the last eight years. Earlier that week, I received an e-mail from Brian Gallagher asking for the time of the event and if it would be okay if he and his sister, Tracy, were to attend. Though we had sent a couple of e-mails back and forth, I hadn't seen Brian since last January when we met for dinner and ice cream.

On this particular night, my friend Carla made a beeline for me while I was focused on greeting our guests for the evening. She had an air of excitement about her as she told me where Brian and Tracy's table was located and urged me to go and say hello.

Brian and I exchanged our polite greetings, but they were cut short after my attention was pulled away by other guests wanting to say hello.

At the banquet, Brian found out that we were moving our pregnancy center to a new location down the road and we needed new offices built. Since he is a master at carpentry and has a generous heart, Brian was one of the first to sign up for this worthy project.

Searching for Happily-Ever-After

A Word from Brian . . .

I decided to attend the annual CPC banquet that year because, after my mom passed away, our family sensed a need to step up and fill in the gaps where she once stood. The CPC was part of that initiative to memorialize one of the passions in her life. Quietly, I was also hoping to see Amber again when my sister and I showed up at the event.

I found out that evening that the Center desperately needed workers to help build in their new location and I was happy to be a part of this venture. I didn't know if this would lead to another encounter with Amber, but I knew I had to do something to help.

New Year's Eve and Family Ties

A Word from Brian . . .

Amber and I kept in touch off and on over the course of that summer via e-mail and before year's end, on New Year's Eve, Amber would come back into my life for good.

* * * *

I showed up at my friend Carla's house around nine o'clock. We had big plans for good food and Jane Austen movies to ring in the 2010 New Year. Once I had arrived, Carla quickly informed me that we were invited to Tracy Esposito's house for games, food, and ball-dropping festivities. Carla seemed really excited and so I agreed to go. It sounded like fun. In the back of my mind I wondered if Brian would also be at his sister's house on this night.

I walked into the New Year's Eve bash and found myself face to face with Mr. Brian Gallagher once again. We all had such a good night of games, laughter, and singing around the piano. I couldn't remember having so much fun.

AMBER GALLAGHER

A Word from Brian . . .

'Cast your bread upon the water and after many days it will return' (Ecclesiastes 11:1). On New Year's Eve, my bread returned. Admittedly, waking up on New Year's Eve morning was kind of a low point for me. I tried to remain optimistic throughout the spring and summer, but now fall had passed and winter was setting in again and the reality of another New Year's Eve alone was hard. Unmotivated, I didn't make plans that year. However, by late afternoon I got a call from my sister saying that she was having a party. She also mentioned that Amber might be coming as well and in an instant my mood turned buoyant. It would be so good to finally see her again.

****

Beyond New Year's Eve, I continued to become fast friends with this family who liked to plan lots of social functions. I later found out that these sweet friends feverishly planned activities so that Brian and I could spend time getting to know each other in a group setting.

A Courtship Begins

Over the next couple of months, Brian and I spent time observing each other interact with our own families and friends. It was not hard to notice that Brian was deeply loved by his brothers, sisters, nieces, nephews, friends, and strangers alike. He was a man of goodness and kindness—a man filled with godly integrity. I kept asking God, "Is he for real?"

1/17/10 Journal Entry

After working at the center, I hung out with Carla and Brian last night. We went out for dinner, then to the grocery store. We went back to Carla's, played Bible Trivia, and had a really good time. Brian walked me to my car and told me that he knew I was in a transition period, but he wanted to get to know me and spend more time together.

Lord, I told him that I was pretty cautious. I needed good friends around me and that rather than hanging out alone, I'd rather hang out in groups of people. Lord, I don't know if I thoroughly confused him. Please help him to understand and if I need to clarify, please put your words in my mouth.

Brian later told me that after this conversation he was pretty discouraged. He had never heard about courtship and so he thought that I was giving him the "let's just be friends" brushoff.

He had begun to distance himself from me when I approached him one evening after he had worked at the pregnancy center. I asked him if he had ever heard of courtship. He said that he hadn't. So, I told him that I wasn't giving him the brushoff, but instead I really did want to get to know him. I simply wanted to do that in the context of a friendship and not a romantic relationship. He seemed relieved and we continued to become better friends.

In February, I ended up winning the big "Family Video Golf Tournament." I had never heard of such an event, but of course, Brian politely insisted on taking me out to a victory dinner. I was excited to go because I had grown to deeply admire this man and I looked forward to spending more time together.

Then in March, my heart turned a corner. Brian's sister's asked me to teach a "Princess Within" retreat for their daughters and some friends. It was an amazing time getting to know this family even better. One of the evenings as we were returning to our hotel after dinner, I decided to do some investigating. I asked Melissa and Tracy to tell me about Brian. They seemed a little shocked. Until this conversation, I had kept any interest in Brian to myself. I wanted to make certain that the Lord was directing me. They shared story after story, every one confirming the integrity and godly devotion Brian consistently portrayed to his friends and family. Several new details about Brian affected me in a way that I had not expected:

AMBER GALLAGHER

3/29/10 Journal Entry

I had an interesting conversation with Brian's sisters and Lord, I found out that Brian not only read 'The Princess Within' Bible study, but he also worked through the questions. They also told me that his mom's sickness with cancer really affected him. He would bring her flowers or a gift each day when he would come to see her. Lord, I am starting to feel really impressed by him. I think I may like him. I am asking You, with praise and thanksgiving, to set a guard over me—that Your peace would guard my heart and mind in Christ Jesus. You are the One that opens and closes doors that no man can open or close.

Lord, when I think about the kindness shown to me by You, I can't help but cry. I am extremely grateful.

Little by little the doors to my heart were opening up to this genuine man of unique character and kindness. He reminded me a lot of my late grandpa, Robert Eugene, whom I adored and knew to be one of the kindest men I had ever encountered. Even more so, Brian reminded me of Jesus. I would catch glimpses in Brian of the One that my heart truly beat for. This was what I had always prayed for in a Christ-like husband, but I knew I had to remain cautious. In previous times, I had fallen in love with the Jesus in people and had mistaken that for falling in love with the actual person. I didn't want to be guilty of that this time. Even if a man loved Jesus, he still might not be God's choice for my future husband.

When I found out that Brian had not only purchased my Bible study, but also worked through it, I was certainly intrigued. "Who does that?" I wondered. Tracy said that Brian wanted to know my heart and he thought that reading *The Princess Within* was one of the best ways to do that. This conversation catapulted my heart into such a depth of fondness toward Brian that I don't ever remember feeling for anyone before.

In April, I went to a convention with the ladies from work. I asked the Lord for direction in this friendship with Brian. Even though I had developed a deep admiration for him, I asked God to close the door for Brian and I if a romance was not His will. On my way back into town, I got a text from Brian: "Can I see you?"

My heart leapt. I hadn't really talked to him all weekend and was trying to prepare myself in case God wanted to abruptly close the door. This was perhaps the night God may have done just that and I didn't want to be holding on too tightly.

We went to dinner and talked for hours. Brian was still struggling his way through understanding the courtship process and that night, the Lord began to bring clarity to him. At one point in our conversation, it seemed as if Heaven were listening in. I felt God powerfully that night as Brian dropped me off at my car. It felt calm and peaceful. It was a sweet ending to a great weekend.

From this point forward, Brian and I began to grow even closer. We were on a mission to determine whether or not we felt God wanted us to marry. One afternoon, it hit me, "On that day back in July, didn't I pray and ask God to bring my husband into my life by the end of the year?"

I realized that Brian Gallagher had come back into my life about three hours before we rang in that New Year. Hmm . . . now that was interesting. I stored this revelation away in my heart and would occasionally allow myself to ponder, "Did God really do it?"

A Word from Brian . . .

We really didn't date in the worldly sense. We took our time and progressed slowly. We got to know each other and I was able to share with Amber all of my failures and successes. I told her how I was committed to not having sex until marriage and miraculously she agreed. Amber shared with me how she wanted to go the second mile and not even kiss until her wedding day, and to that I replied 'Let's not get crazy' but somehow, I agreed.

I remember one summer day sitting there with Amber, completely at ease, having just bared my soul. During that moment, God said to me, 'For the first time in your life, you are in love the way that I have designed it.'

AMBER GALLAGHER

Since then I have concluded that for a man, it is impossible to know his true feelings about a woman until sex is removed completely from his motivation. And for a woman, she will never truly know how a man feels about her until all sexual activity is saved for the day an eternal covenant is made.

True Love and Carriage Rides

As Brian and I continued to grow closer, I persisted in praying for God's direction, eventually easing into a comfortable "knowing" in my heart. There was no anxiety or fear. Instead, peace settled over me like a warm blanket. I began to write prayers in my journal that said, "Lord, I feel as though Brian is the one I am to marry."

A Parent's Blessing

On June 26, 2010, I was away at another conference when Brian made a visit to my father. While he was outside asking for my dad's blessing for us to be married, my mom was excitedly calling me on the phone, "Guess who is here right now?"

She gave me a play by play as her and my grandma peeked out and giggled like little girls trying to listen in.

Sure enough, dad told Brian that they were behind us one hundred percent. Oh, what a joy to have such approval and support. It really gave our hearts courage to move in the direction that we felt God leading us.

A Word from Brian . . .

Once I became aware of my true feelings for Amber, and having also received God's approval, I was able to move forward with confidence. Even though I felt assurance in my heart, I still wanted to respect tradition and tell Amber's Dad of my intentions concerning his daughter and ask for his blessing. While some of the minor details escape me, it was one of the easiest things that I have ever done.

I recall going into detail about how I loved his daughter and how well she was raised. I also told Amber's Dad how much I wanted to look after his little girl and take care of her for the rest of her life. I concluded by saying that in lieu of receiving permission to marry his daughter, I would much rather receive his blessing instead.

A big smile creased his face as he understood my heart and graciously gave his blessing. Words can't describe the level of pleasure and happiness I felt in that moment—to be freely given the mantle of another man's one and only daughter is a privilege unspeakable.

Will You Marry Me?

A Word from Brian . . .

After a long weekend of basking in a father's blessing, reality started to set in. How does a guy pop the question in a way befitting a Princess? She has a royal pedigree, while I have the grace of a rugby playing barbarian in comparison. Not to panic, though, I comforted myself with the notion that my daily bread for gaining nuptial insight would be given so that Amber would be able to experience her lifelong dream. Not that everything had to be perfect, but let's face it, every woman dreams of her proposal and wedding day and I wanted to make her dreams come true.

The ring I ended up buying couldn't be just any ring, it had to be one designed for a Princess. After much deliberation, I ended up with something that more closely represents her vintage elegance. I have to admit that I felt relief after I popped the question and found her boisterous approval.

In researching ways to propose, I realized that Amber most probably had one reoccurring dream for that most treasured day. I struggled. The barbarian inside of me brought me to a park in Cincinnati where I used to play rugby. It had a great view overlooking the city with the centerpiece of the park being a medieval style castle pavilion built in the early 1900's and at sunset during a beautiful summer day, I convinced myself that this was the place to propose to a modern-day Princess.

****

Thursday, July 1, 2010, will be one of the most memorable days of my life. I was getting off of work early to meet Brian. We were having an official "Fun Day." These are days spent entirely on enjoying fun, out-of-the-ordinary excursions.

We headed to Cincinnati, first stopping to eat at the Cheesecake Factory. Brian was so eager, perhaps even a little giddy. I thought, "Wow! He is really enthusiastic about leaving work early today."

After lunch, we headed downtown for some shopping and exploring. We tried to see the local IMAX movie at the old Union Terminal, but would have to wait until later that evening for another available showing. As the night wore on, we landed at Boston Market for dinner and afterward Brian said he wanted to show me the beautiful Ault Park. I love nature and flowers and had never been there before. I agreed without hesitation.

7/1/10 Journal Entry

Brian told me that he was originally going to propose to me where the stone castle structure looks out over the city at Ault Park. He reasoned, 'The sun sets beautifully there.' As it turns out, a wedding party was having their reception and the castle was closed to outsiders. So, instead, we walked around the park and took pictures. It was beautiful.

After our park excursion, Brian mentioned that we had seen some horse and carriages earlier in the day. "Would you like to take a pony ride?"

"Sure!" I eagerly replied, oblivious to the fact that I was going to be thankful I had accidently left a camera in my purse.

Within the half hour, we were climbing into our carriage drawn by a horse named, of all things, *Prince*. Mr. Richey, our driver, with his down-home twang, recited the history of Cincinnati as we trotted along. Midway through our tour, we turned down Garfield Street, which was named after President Garfield because his former residence was located there. As though he were taking stage direction from God, Mr. Richey paused in front of a beautiful church, which illuminated as if the glory of God were bursting through its majestic structure. The sight was quite breathtaking. I immediately dug into my purse and pulled out my camera to try and capture the moment. I felt Brian shuffle next to me.

"Seeing that church has got me thinking that I need to figure out how I'm going to propose. I'd probably get down on one knee like this (Brian had lowered to his knee.) . . . and I'd probably reach into my pocket like this . . . and I would pull out a box like this . . ." He teased.

I gasped, "What are you doing, honey?"

". . . and if I was going to propose, I'd probably have a ring like this." He continued as he opened up the little brown box to reveal the ring that I had previously seen and loved at the jewelry store.

My mind was racing. "Is he still practicing or is this for real?"

Brian went on to say, "Amber, I love you and I want to spend the rest of my life with you."

"YES!" I cried out . . . a little premature. The excitement was gloriously overwhelming.

"Will you marry me?" he chuckled.

"YES!"

We were as excited as two little kids on Christmas morning. We chattered and laughed and hugged. On the final leg of our horse and carriage tour, I had a revelation.

"Oh my goodness!" I said.

"What?" Brian was a little startled.

"Well, I've never told you this, but my dream has always been to have a carriage ride proposal. I have for years told a story as part of my junior high classroom presentation about a couple who sets boundaries, develops a healthy relationship, and falls in love. When the young man in the story proposes, he does so by taking the young lady on a carriage ride around the city. This was a story that I made up, but it was always the proposal I had hoped for one day."

"Wow, you never told me that. I was going to do something totally different for this night," Brian replied in amazement.

"That is what makes this so wonderful! The Holy Spirit is right here, guiding us."

I knew that this moment had God's beautiful hands all over it. We were escorted the rest of the way in awe of the divine setup we had just encountered.

Several days later, I felt the Lord speak to my heart, "Amber, I heard every time you told that story to those kids. I knew your heart's desire and I knew what I was going to do for you when you did not. At times you questioned and wondered if I had forgotten you. I heard every word and I was planning all the while for you. I did not forget you."

Our Carriage Ride

Celebrating Our Engagement

30

A God-Sized Tale

Every person's life is a fairytale written by God's fingers.

-Hans Christian Anderson

'For I know the plans that I have for you,' declares the Lord, 'plans to prosper you and not to harm you, plans to give you hope and a future.' (Jeremiah 29:11 NIV)

A Word from Brian . . .

I had a genuine sense of fulfillment when I woke up on the morning of my wedding day and it came to a climax when the barn doors opened and in stepped my bride.

* * * *

It took place on October twenty-third. It was a beautiful, warm fall day. The leaves proudly showed all of their colors as they adorned our Saturday afternoon wedding in a way that could never be manufactured. God fulfilled one of my greatest dreams. I was privileged to marry the one my heart loves, Brian Robert Gallagher.

We decided to exchange our vows on my brother-in-law's farm. That day, the two hundred-year-old barn's cathedral ceiling radiated with thousands of twinkling lights. The atmosphere was rugged and simple with a touch of elegance gleaming from the candlelight of linen-covered tables. The entire venue was graced with fall flowers of every hue while wrought-iron pumpkin carriages and glass-slipper place cards presented a backdrop for my own God-sized tale.

It was an intimate affair. There was no need for a massive congregation. Simply gathered were our closest family and friends as they crowded wall to wall to see not only our prayers but theirs being answered on this day. I can't help but wonder if there was also "a great cloud of witnesses" peeking in to celebrate this sacred occasion.

At the foot of the altar, Brian had purchased a massive garden stone which he said would "forever mark the place in which we stood to say our vows." Engraved on the stone were our names along with the phrase, "This stone will stand as a memorial forever," just as the children of Israel proclaimed when they finally entered into *their* promised land (Joshua 4:7). Brian affectionately joked, "One day, when we are old and gray, we will tell our grandchildren that on top of this memorial stone was the very place where your grandma and I got married."

Sure enough, as we stood before the Lord on top of that symbolic stone, Brian and I vowed our lasting covenant. It felt as if God was smiling on us like a proud Papa and then . . . we sealed our sacred ceremony with a long-awaited kiss! We feasted, laughed, and celebrated like two sojourners who were finally home, staking their place in a divine "Promised Land." I felt an indescribable joy as we left the barn escorted by a Belgian horse-drawn carriage.

On our wedding night, I gave my husband a book of letters and prayers that I had written throughout the years. Some of those letters were written on nights when I was struggling to keep heart as I waited to see what God was going to do, but this night was not one of those nights.

Instead my heart was bursting with joy. The Lord had orchestrated a tale that took my breath away. When He moves in such a miraculous display, something about it feels as if for a moment, all is right in the world. His kingdom has come, for a time, "on Earth as it is in Heaven." There is a sense of peace, comfort, and beauty. Yes, it feels a bit like home to me.

The First Look

God did it!

Searching for Happily-Ever-After

Now that's joy. I love this picture.

Happily-Ever-After

An Epilogue

Those who look to Him for help will be radiant with joy; no shadow of shame will darken their faces. (Psalm 34:5 NLT)

As I write this, I have been married for two years and love it. I still marvel and thank God for doing what only He could. Last Christmas, a dear friend gave me the beautiful gift of a wrought-iron birdcage with the sweetest little bird perched inside. I brought it home and showed Brian. The next thing I knew, I heard my inventive husband in the garage with his grinder saw tool. "As usual, he must be working on a new project," I thought. About a half an hour later, Brian came back into the house with a smile on his face. He presented my previous birdcage gift, only it had definitely been altered. Instead of being perched inside on its ledge, Brian had removed the little bird and fastened it on top of the cage as if it were ready to take flight. "She's out of the cage," he declared. I nodded and smiled, "Yes!" I knew exactly what he meant. Man, I love that guy!

I am often brought to tears of gratitude because when I get an e-mail or phone call from a struggling lady-in-waiting, I can recall in an instant that all-too-familiar ache. My heart goes out to her and in those times, I cannot help but recount what God has done.

I know that my waiting story is not merely for me. I believe God wrote it for anyone who is in waiting. My story is simply one of the many examples of The Great Legacy Love Affair at work in a person's life. There are many different versions to this narrative describing God's faithfulness. May you recognize that you are in the midst of your very own adventure right now. I wonder if you will choose to step into this divine tale with God. Will you press through and perhaps even come to enjoy your time in the waiting? I encourage you not to lose heart. Sure, every story has some unexpected turns in the adventure of it all, but please don't ever forget that He means to give you an "expected end" (Jeremiah 29:11).

Your story will be completely worth the wait, but even more than what God will do for you, remember that He has already offered you happily-ever-after in your love affair with Him—the Heavenly Prince. He alone is the fulfillment of all that any of us have ever longed for whether single or married and until we surrender to that truth, happiness will continue to elude us. I will often say to a waiting lady, "It's when you are content in the relationship between Jesus and you, that you just might be ready." I say this because it is precisely what the Lord made clear to this lady-in-waiting who writes to you now.

The same God, who I imagine asked His disciple with such humility and longing, "Peter, do you love Me?" (John 6:68) is perhaps asking you now, "Do you love Me? Will you wait for Me? Will you trust Me and wait to see what I will do in all My creativity and splendor? Will you hold out when the world pressures you to give in?" God knows what the wait is all about—the ache and the longing, because He has patiently and longingly waited for you. He is not asking of you anything that He has not done Himself. Oh, did you not know? You are *His* Happily-Ever-After.

He saw the joy ahead of him, so he endured death on the cross and ignored the disgrace it brought him. (Hebrews 12:2b GWT)

That "joy ahead of Him" was you. It has been His heart from the very beginning to be with you—the one that He so extravagantly loves. How thrilling! So, dear Lady-in-Waiting, may you wait well and enjoy your journey into Happily-Ever-After.

Let us not become weary in doing good, for at the proper time we will reap a harvest if we don't give up. (Galatians 6:9 NIV 1984)

Wait patiently for the LORD. Be brave and courageous. Yes, wait patiently for the LORD. (Psalm 27:14 NLT)

But if we look forward to something we don't yet have, we must wait patiently and confidently. (Romans 8:25 NLT)

I wait for the LORD, my soul waits, and in his word I put my hope. (Psalm 130:5 NIV 1984)

Endnotes

Introduction:

1. Michael Warden. *Alone with God: Biblical Inspiration for the Unmarried*. (Ohio: Barbour Publishing, Inc. 2002), 255.

Chapter Five:

1. Robert Frost. "The Road Not Taken." *Mountain Interval.* New York: Henry Holt and Company, 1920; Bartleby.com, 1999. www.bartleby.com/119/. [Accessed February 19, 2013].
2. "Tracing the Steps of Paul." Truth in History. http://www.truthinhistory.org/tracing-the-steps-of-the-apostle-paul.html. [Accessed March 8, 2012].

Chapter Six:

1. Blue Letter Bible. "Dictionary and Word for qavah (Strong's 6960)." http://www.blueletterbible.org/lang/lexicon/lexicon.cfm?Strongs=H6960&t=KJV. [Accessed March 21, 2012].
2. Strong's Concordance with Greek and Hebrew Lexicon. http://www.eliyah.com/cgi-bin/strongs.cgi?file=hebrewlexicon&isindex=sharath, Strong's #8334. [Accessed March 21, 2013].
3. Blue Letter Bible. "Dictionary and Word Search for tsaphah (Strong's 6822)." http:// www.blueletterbible.org/lang/lexicon/lexicon.cfm? Strongs=H6822&t=KJV. [Accessed March 21, 2012].

Chapter Seven:

1. Trent Reznor/Performed by Johnny Cash. "Hurt." Albums: American IV: The Man Comes Around-2003. Unearthed-2003, The Legend of Johnny Cash-2005, et al.
2. Becky Tirabassi. *Let Prayer Change Your Life.* Tennessee: Thomas Nelson, Inc., 1990, 1992, 2000.
3. Mentor. www.dictionary.com Unabridged, [Accessed March 27, 2012].

Chapter Nine:

1. Elisabeth Elliot. *The Journals of Jim Elliot.* Michigan: Revell, 1978.

Chapter Ten:

1. Sibusiso Ntsala. "Moving with the Lamb." North America: Vineyard Songs (SA). Admin. by Mercy/Vineyard Publishing (ASCAP), 1999.

Chapter Twelve:

1. Blue Letter Bible. "Dictionary and Word Search for *yare' (Strong's 3372)*". Blue Letter Bible. 1996-2013. http://www.blueletterbible.org/lang/lexicon/lexicon.cfm?Strongs=H3372&t=KJV. [Accessed March 25, 2013].
2. Joe S. McIlhaney and Freda McKissic Bush. *Hooked: New Science on How Casual Sex is Affecting Our Children.* (Illinois: Northfield Publishing, 2008), 37.
3. McIlhaney and Bush. *Hooked,* 41.
4. McIlhaney and Bush. *Hooked,* 43.
5. "The Majority of High School Students Have Remained Abstinent." www.familyfacts.org. Centers for Disease Control

and Prevention, National Youth Risk Behavior Survey, 2011. [Accessed February 21, 2013].
6. "Teenage Pregnancy." March of Dimes. www.marchofdimes.com/professionals/25079_1159.asp. [Accessed February 21, 2013]. Originally Published in Hamilton, B.E., et al. Births: Preliminary Data for 2007. National Vital Statistics Report, volume 57, number 12, March 18, 2009.
7. Angie Vineyard. "Protection Teens are not Getting: The Staggering Epidemic of Teen STDs," [Accessed February 21, 2013]. Originally published Concerned Women for America. www.beverlylahayeinstitute.org/articledisplay.asp?id=2944&department=BLI&categoryid=femfacts, 2002.
8. Jennifer Roback Morse. "The Problem With Living Together." www.focusonthefamily.com/marriage/preparing_for_marriage/test_driving_marriage/the_problem_with_living_together.aspx. [Accessed February 22, 2013].
9. Bruce Cook. "Sex and Alcohol Don't Mix." *Choosing the Best Life*. Georgia: Choosing the Best, Inc., 2000.
10. John Eldredge and Stasi Eldredge. *Captivating: Unveiling the Mystery of a Woman's Soul*. Tennessee: Thomas Nelson, Inc., 2005, 2010.
11. Linda J. Waite and Maggie Gallagher, *The Case for Marriage: Why Married People Are Happier, Healthier and Better off Financially*. New York: Crown Publishing Group, 2001.

Chapter Thirteen:

1. Pure. http://www.merriam-webster.com/dictionary/pure. [Accessed February 21, 2013].

Chapter Fourteen:

1. W. Phillip Keller. *A Shepherd Looks at Psalm 23*. (Michigan: Zondervan, 1970, 2007), 138-139.

2. Excerpt from Wickipedia: "Βεελζεβούλ, ὁ indecl. (v.l. Βεελζεβούβ and Βεεζεβούλ W-S. §5, 31, cp. 27 n. 56) Beelzebul, orig. a Philistine deity; the name בּוּב זְ לְ ע.בּ means Baal (lord) of flies (4 Km 1:2, 6; Sym. transcribes βεελζεβούβ; Vulgate Beelzebub; TestSol freq. Βεελζεβούλ,-βουέλ)." Arndt, W., Danker, F. W., & Bauer, W. (2000). A Greek-English lexicon of the New Testament and other early Christian literature (3rd ed.) (173). Chicago: University of Chicago Press.
3. "Barnes' Notes on the Bible (Genesis 1:20-21, Genesis 1:24)." Bible Suite. www.bible.cc/genesis/2-7.htm. [Accessed February 21, 2013].
4. Entice. www.audioenglish.net/dictionary/entice.htm [Accessed February 21, 2013].
5. Keller. *A Shepherd Looks at Psalm 23*.

Chapter Fifteen:

1. "Herod's Temple." http://www.bible-history.com/jewishtemple [Accessed February 24, 2013].
2. Blue Letter Bible. "Dictionary and Word Search for 'hagiasmos' (Strong's 38)." Blue Letter Bible. 1996-2012. 29 http://www.blueletterbible.org/lang/lexicon/lexicon.cfm?Strongs=G38&t=KJV. [Accessed February 22, 2013].
3. "Hagiasmos." Bible Suite. www.biblesuite.com/greek/38/htm. [Accessed February 22, 2013].
4. Blue Letter Bible. "Dictionary and Word Search for 'Hagiazo' (Strong's 37)." Blue Letter Bible. 1996-2013. http://www.blueletterbible.org/lang/lexicon/Lexicon.cfm?Strongs=G&t=KJV. [Accessed February 21, 2013].
5. "A Systematic Study of Bible Doctrine: The Doctrine of Sanctification." www.pbministries.org/Theology/Simmons/chapter27.htm. [Accessed February 21, 2013].
6. David Palmer. "Be Holy for I Am Holy." Beyond Today: Understanding Your Future. www.ucg.org/christian-living/be-holy-i-am-holy/. [Accessed February 21, 2013].

7. "Kodesh Hakadoshim." www.hebrew4christians.com/Glossary/Hebrew_Gossary_-_K/hebrew_glossary_-_k.html. [Accessed February 22, 2013].

Chapter Eighteen:

1. "Prophet." www.christiananswers.net/dictionary/prophet.html. [Accessed February 21, 2013].
2. Michael Warden. *Alone with God: Biblical Inspiration for the Unmarried.* (Ohio: Barbour Publishing, Inc. 2002), 201.

Chapter Nineteen:

1. John Eldredge. *The Journey of Desire: Searching for the Life We've Only Dreamed Of.* (Tennessee: Thomas Nelson, Inc, 2000), 23.
2. "Why Do Some Trees Lose Their Leaves?" www.wisegeek.com/why-do-some-trees-lose-their-leaves, USDA Forest Service: www.na.fs.fed.us/fhp/pubs/leaves/leaves.shtm [Accessed February 24, 2013].
3. Beth Moore. *James: Mercy Triumphs.* Tennessee: LifeWay Press, 2011.
4. Nancy Leigh DeMoss. *Lies Women Believe and the Truth That Sets Them Free.* (Chicago: Moody Publishers, 2001), 264-265.
5. Stormie Omartian. *Just Enough Light for the Step I'm On: Trusting God in the Tough Times.* Oregon: Harvest House Publishers, 1999, 2008.

Chapter Twenty-One:

1. Brent Curtis and John Eldredge. *The Sacred Romance: Drawing Closer to the Heart of God.* Tennessee: Thomas Nelson, Inc., 1997.
2. John Eldredge. *The Journey of Desire: Searching for the Life We've Only Dreamed Of.* Tennessee: Thomas Nelson, Inc., 2000.

Chapter Twenty-Two:

1. Stormie Omartian. *Just Enough Light for the Step I'm On: Trusting God in the Tough Times*. Oregon: Harvest House Publishers, 1999, 2008.
2. Omartian. *Just Enough Light for the Step I'm On*.

Chapter Twenty-Three:

1. Beth Moore. *Esther: It's Tough Being a Woman*. Tennessee: LifeWay Press, Released 2008. DVD.

Chapter Twenty-Four:

1. Michael Warden. *Alone with God: Biblical Inspiration for the Unmarried*. Ohio: Barbour Publishing, Inc. 2002.
2. Janet Folger. *What's a Girl to Do? While Waiting for Mr. Right*. Oregon: Multnomah Publishers, Inc., 2004.
3. Beth Moore. *Esther: It's Tough Being a Woman*. Tennessee: LifeWay Press, 2008.

Chapter Twenty-Seven:

1. Beth Moore. *Esther: It's Tough Being a Woman*. Tennessee: LifeWay Press, 2008.

About Amber Gallagher

Amber Gallagher, the founder of Sacred Revolution Ministries, is a passionate writer, singer, and public speaker.

For over a decade, she has directed The Positive Life Choices Education Program for The Community Pregnancy Center (www.pregnancychoice.net) and has spoken to over 75,000 young men and women on the topics of abstinence, character, and healthy relationships.

Amber has previously authored two Bible studies, *The Princess Within: Living Like a Princess from the Inside Out* and *The Sacred Revolution: Uncovering Purity for the Modern-Day Knight*.

Amber has also addressed numerous women's groups as she shares her personal and oftentimes humorous life experience in an effort to nurture the hearts of ladies of all ages.

To learn more about Amber or to schedule her to speak at your event, go to www.sacredrevolt.com.

On a Mission . . .

Sacred Revolution Ministries was founded in 2008 with a passion "to inspire and equip people for the sacred life with Christ."

This frontline ministry offers resources to help individuals cultivate a genuine and ever-growing relationship with God.

Visit us online at:

www.princesswithin.com   www.sacredrevolt.com

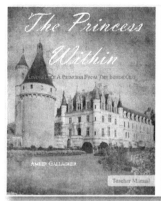 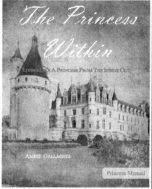

The Princess Within

Living Like a Princess from the Inside Out

This unique Bible study is designed to be used in any number of ways. Perhaps a five-day "Princess Camp," Bible study or weekend retreat is just what you've been looking for. Another great aspect is that this study can be tailored for any audience. It has successfully been implemented for elementary, middle, high school, and adult women's groups.

Through this life-changing study, ladies will embark on an amazing adventure with God as they travel through each session covering topics such as "The Great Legacy Love Affair," "The Qualities of a True Princess," "What to Look for in a Prince," "The Purity of a Princess" and "Building a Castle of Dreams."

What Are Ladies Saying?

"After living through many [of my parents'] divorces, and being abused so many times, my heart grew hard and cold. God spoke through your stories and showed me that romance is real, and sex can be beautiful (in proper context)."

"Hearing about the depth of God's love and how much He treasures us, was completely mind blowing."

Let's get back to the real story playing out here—a story with a kingdom in turmoil awaiting the rightful King to demolish the invading enemy forces and return the captive people to peace and prosperity. This King Jesus is currently building His revolutionary army. Are you in?

The Sacred Revolution

Uncovering Purity for the Modern-Day Knight

The Sacred Revolution: Uncovering Purity for the Modern-Day Knight Bible study will help to lead young men on a journey to reclaim their God-given destiny as sons of the Most High God. This study offers an eye-opening look at the importance of purity and holiness as well as strategies of war for conquering temptation and setting boundary lines for maintaining a victorious and flourishing relationship with God.

This curriculum can be used as a personal Bible study or as material for a class/retreat setting and is designed for any young man determined to grow in righteous manhood, integrity, and purity.

It is sure to be a worthy adventure!

CPSIA information can be obtained at www.ICGtesting.com
Printed in the USA
BVOW082003240613

324166BV00001B/1/P